DEVELOPING AND DIRECTING COUNSELOR EDUCATION LABORATORIES

Proceedings of an ACES National Conference Think Tank

DEVELOPING AND DIRECTING COUNSELOR EDUCATION LABORATORIES

Proceedings of an ACES National Conference Think Tank

Jane E. Myers
Editor

AMERICAN COUNSELING ASSOCIATION

Developing and Directing Counselor Education Laboratories

10 9 8 7 6 5 4 3 2 1

American Counseling Association
5999 Stevenson Avenue
Alexandria, VA 22304

Director of Communications
Jennifer L. Sacks

Acquisitions and Development Editor
Carolyn Baker

Production/Design Manager
Michael Comlish

Copyeditor
Heather Jefferson

Cover design by Martha Woolsey

Library of Congress Cataloging-in-Publication Data

Developing and directing counselor education laboratories :
    proceedings of an ACES national conference think tank / Jane E. Myers, editor.
      p. cm.
    Papers from a think tank at the national conference of the Association for
    Counselor Education and Supervision held in Sept. 1992 in San Antonio, Tex.
    Includes bibliographical references.
    ISBN 1-55620-137-0
    1. Counseling—Study and teaching—Congresses. 2. Counselors—Training of—
Congresses. I. Myers, Jane E. II. Association for Counselor Education and Supervision.
BF637.C6D478   1994
361.3'23'0711—dc20   94-3946
                                                                          CIP

TABLE OF CONTENTS

PREFACE

In the fall of 1991, I was assigned to direct the counselor education clinic (laboratory) at the University of North Carolina at Greensboro. Alfred Smith was hired as a graduate assistant 20 hours per week to assist me in operating our already established clinic. I immediately called for help from people like Rex Stockton, Al Dye, Mike Altekruse, and Rick Wantz who had been directing clinics for years. It quickly became apparent that there was no existing forum within the Association for Counselor Education and Supervision (ACES) to promote dialogue among counselor education clinic directors. ACES was receptive to the establishment of such a network, which was accomplished under the leadership of President Harold Hackney.

In preparation for our first network meeting in Baltimore in March 1992, Al Smith and I (network co-chairs) conducted a literature search for information regarding on-campus clinical training of counselors, and prepared a paper summarizing what we could find and the implications for counselor education. The original title of that paper ("Counselor Education Clinics: Opportunities, Obstacles, and Options") became the focus of a seven-session think tank on counselor education clinics, which was conducted at the national ACES conference in San Antonio in September 1992. The topics for the sessions were identified through brainstorming among network members concerning the critical issues in on-campus clinical training. Each of the sessions included two or more prepared papers and one or more reactions, all by invited presenters identified through the network as having expertise relative to counselor-training clinics. The papers from the think tank have been prepared for publication in this book, which is the proceedings of the first national think tank on counselor education training clinics.

One of the first difficulties encountered in addressing the issues related to training clinics relates to definitions. The Council for Accreditation of Counseling and Related Educational Programs (CACREP) standards, although specifying the need for clinical training in counselor education, fail to clearly distinguish between requirements for a physical facility and requirements for the actual operation of a counseling clinic, which is part of a counselor education program. The standards include brief definitions of *clinical training* and *counseling laboratory* (see Appendices A and B), yet little guidance is provided to counselor education programs to assist them in addressing the multiple and complex roles of an on-campus clinic.

The first chapter of this book, orginally prepared as the background working paper for the San Antonio think tank, includes a review of the available published literature concerning training clinics. Because the counseling literature includes little or no such references, literaure in the field of psychology training is reviewed and implications for counselor education are considered. It is recognized that there may be unique aspects of on-campus training of counselors that contribute to preparation issues not considered in the psychology literature.

Part I includes three chapters related to the CACREP standards for clinical training. In chapter 2, Joe Wittmer (CACREP's first executive director) provides a historical context for the evolution of the clinical standards, providing examples and quotes from Bob Stripling's original handwritten papers. Wittmer concludes that the original intent of training laboratories was to provide a prepracticum experience, not to be used for practicum or internships that were to be conducted on-site in community agencies. In chapter 3, Carol Bobby (the current executive director of CACREP) and Joseph Kandor (the current chair of CACREP) provide an overview of the CACREP clinical standards and their meaning for counselor education programs seeking accreditation by CACREP. In chapter 4, Thomas Sweeney (CACREP's first chair) reflects on the "spirit" of the standards and discusses challenges to counselor education programs in implementing the standards with a goal toward excellence in professional preparation.

One of the most important aspects of the operation of a clinic is the role of the director. In part II, three experienced clinic directors provide an in-depth analysis of the responsibilities of clinic directors. In chapters 5 and 6, respectively, Richard Wantz, a clinic director for more than 15 years, and Rex Stockton, a director for more than 16 years, each provide a unique perspective on the job description of a clinic director. In chapter 7, Susan DeVaney, a counselor educator about to launch a career as a clinic director, reacts to Wantz and Stockton from a "newcomer's" perspective. In chapter 8, Roger Hutchinson, a clinic director for over 15 years, provides additional insights into the challenging roles of the director.

Legal and ethical issues are reviewed in part III. Theodore Remley, an attorney and professional counselor, discusses legal aspects of operating an on-campus clinic in chapter 9. In chapter 10, Robert Pate focuses on the many ethical dilemmas that result when training is provided on campus, noting quite accurately that there are many more questions than answers in this area. This part concludes with a reaction from Brooke Collison, former chair of the ACA Insurance Trust (chapter 11).

On-campus entry-level training (e.g., prepracticum and practicum) are considered in part IV. Allan Dye reviews the nature of the on-campus practicum in chapter 12, arguing succinctly for direct supervision of counselors in training by counselor educators rather than field supervisors. In chapter 13, Susan Neufeldt provides an overview of her experiences in a graduate training clinic; she emphasizes that the client population is identical to what counselors in the field will encounter, and discusses the implications for training when "real-life" clients are seen by trainees in the clinic. In the final chapter (chapter 14) of this part, Peggy Smith provides a few reactions to the chapters by Dye and Neufeldt.

Part V provides a close look at training of doctoral-level supervisors in the on-campus clinic. Allan Dye, director of the training clinic at Purdue University for over 17 years, provides an in-depth review of the Purdue program, considering both advantages and disadvantages of their training model (chapter 15). Chapter 16, by John West, Donald Bubenzer, and David Delmonico, provides a similar review of the training program at Kent State University. In chapter 17, Janine Bernard reacts from the perspective of a clinical supervisor, noting the strengths and limitations of doctoral-level training of clinical supervisors.

In part VI, the dual role of the on-campus clinic as a mental health agency is discussed. In chapter 18, George Leddick describes the clinic at Indiana University–Purdue University at Fort Wayne as an example of how a clinic may provide community service in addition to its primary function as a training facility. In chapter 19, Michael Altekruse and Judith Seiters describe the cooperative, university-wide training clinic at Southern Illinois University, noting the advantages of interprofessional collaboration that result from this approach. In the final chapter of this part, Gerald Hutchinson and I react to the preceding two chapters while simultaneously considering the potential conflicts that arise from the dual role created when client services and training are both part of the mission of a clinic—a situation that almost always is the case.

In the concluding chapter (chapter 21), Joseph Rotter reflects on the importance of this book and its contents for counselor education. He summarizes the "next steps" required to implement the many recommendations of the other authors that could, if followed, result in a higher quality of clinical training. On-campus clinical training is both an integral and critical area of counselor training. This book sets the stage for the future in providing a state-of-the-art document relative to counseling laboratories. With hope, the issues raised here will lead to better counselor training in the future.

—Jane E. Myers

ACKNOWLEDGMENTS

Appreciation is due and must be expressed to ACES President Joan England for her support of the think tank, and to the 1992 ACES conference co-chairs, Loretta Bradley and Courtland Lee. Special thanks are due to Don C. Locke, Joe Rotter, and Carole Minor for chairing think-tank sessions. The think-tank presenters, chairs, and reactors who provided the text of their carefully prepared chapters for this book have made a valuable contribution to counselor preparation. Al Smith was a major contributor to the development of the think tank, serving as co-chair of the ACES Directors of Clinical Training and Clinics Interest Network.

ABOUT THE EDITOR

Jane E. Myers, PhD, CRC, NCC, LPCC is a professor of Counselor Education at the University of North Carolina at Greensboro (UNCG), and director of Counseling and Consulting Services, the UNCG on-campus training clinic. She served as president of the American Association for Counseling and Development (AACD), now the American Counseling Association, in 1990–1991. She has been president of two AACD divisions, the Association for Measurement and Evaluation in Counseling and Development (now the Association for Assessment in Counseling) and the Association for Adult Development and Aging, for which she served as founding president. She also served as president of Chi Sigma Iota, the International Counseling Honor Society.

Dr. Myers has been an officer, member, and committee chair for national and division committees of several AACD divisions, including Association for Adult Development and Aging (AADA), Association for Measurement and Evaluation in Counseling and Development (AMECD), the Association for Counselor Education and Supervision (ACES), and the American Rehabilitation Counseling Association (ARCA). She has been the founding co-chair of the ACES Directors of Clinical Training and Clinics Interest Network since 1991.

She has written and edited numerous publications, including 12 books and monographs, over 50 refereed journal articles, and more than 30 additional publications. In addition, she co-produced seven training videotapes for gerontological counseling. Her most recent books include *Adult Children and Aging Parents* and *Empowerment for Later Life*. Dr. Myers has lectured and consulted nationally and internationally and has received numerous awards, including the AACD Research Award, the AACD Arthur A. Hitchcock Distinguished Professional Service Award, and the Gilbert and Kathleen Wrenn Humanitarian and Caring Person Award.

CONTRIBUTORS

Michael K. Altekruse, EdD is currently a professor in the Department of Counselor Education at the University of Nevada at Las Vegas. He was coordinator of psychological services at the Southern Illinois University Clinical Center from 1986 to 1992, and is presently coordinator of the Client Services Center at the University of Nevada at Las Vegas. He is a past president of ACES.

Janine M. Bernard, PhD, NCC is a professor of counselor education in the Graduate School of Education and Allied Professions at Fairfield University in Fairfield, Connecticut. She supervises both practicum and internship students and trains field supervisors in supervision methods and processes.

Carol L. Bobby, PhD, NCC is the executive director of CACREP, Alexandria, Virginia. She has held this position for over 6 years.

Donald L. Bubenzer, PhD, LPCC is a professor in the Counseling and Human Development Service Program at Kent State University in Kent, Ohio. He has supervised students in the program's clinic for 4 years.

Brooke B. Collison, PhD, NCC, LPC is an associate professor of counselor education in the School of Education at Oregon State University in Corvallis. He served as chair of the ACA Insurance Trust from 1989 to 1992. He is a past president of ACA.

David L. Delmonico, MEd is a student supervisor and has been a practicum student in the Kent State counselor education training clinic.

Susan B. DeVaney, EdD, NCC is an assistant professor in the Department of Educational Leadership at Western Kentucky University in Bowling Green.

Allan Dye, PhD is a professor and chair of the Graduate Counseling Program at Rollins College in Winter Park, Florida. He was a faculty member in counselor education at Purdue University from 1964 to 1991, and served as director of the Purdue Counseling and Guidance Center from 1974 to 1991. He is currently establishing a separate on-campus counseling facility at Rollins College, which will accommodate on-campus practica.

Gerald H. Hutchinson, MEd, NCC is a doctoral student in counselor education at the University of North Carolina at Greensboro. He has been assistant clinic director for 2 years and co-chair of the ACES Directors of Clinical Training and Clinics Interest Network beginning in 1993.

Roger L. Hutchinson, EdD, NCC is a professor of counseling psychology at Ball State University. He developed a counselor education training lab in 1969, and directed it for 19 years.

Joseph R. Kandor, EdD, NCC is a professor and chair in the Department of Counselor Education at the State University of New York at Brockport. He is currently chair of the CACREP Board of Directors, a position he has held for 6 years.

George R. Leddick, PhD, NCC, CMFT is an associate professor of education and coordinator of counselor education at Indiana University–Purdue University Fort Wayne (IPFW). He is the founder of the IPFW Counselor Education Clinic and co-author of the *Handbook of Counseling Supervision.*

Susan Allstetter Neufeldt, PhD is director of the Ray E. Hosford Clinic in the Clinical/Counseling/School Psychology Program in the Graduate School of Education at the University of California at Santa Barbara. Prior to 1990, she was in private practice.

Robert H. Pate, Jr., PhD, NCC, LPC is a professor of counselor education and chair of the Department of Human Services at the University of Virginia in Charlottesville. He was one of the originators of, and has at various times served as the faculty supervisor of, the University of Virginia Personal and Career Develop Center, the clinic operated by the Counselor Education Program.

Theodore P. Remley, Jr., JD, PhD is executive director of the American Counseling Association, headquartered in Alexandria, Virginia. He is a counselor educator who, as chair of a CACREP-accredited training program, was instrumental in restructuring the counselor-training clinic at Mississippi State University.

Joseph C. Rotter, EdD, NCC, LPCS is a professor and chair of the Department of Educational Psychology at the University of South Carolina in Columbia. He is a past president of ACES.

Judith Seiters, PhD is director of the Clinical Center at Southern Illinois University in Carbondale.

Alfred W. Smith, MSEd is a doctoral student in counselor education at the University of North Carolina at Greensboro. He was assistant clinic director during 1991–1992, and co-chair of the ACES Directors of Clinical Training and Clinics Interest Network.

Peggy H. Smith, PhD is an associate professor in the Department of Counseling at San Francisco State University. She has been associated with counselor training clinics since 1968, first as a student at Stanford University and then as a faculty member at the University of California at Santa Barbara and SFSU.

Rex Stockton, EdD, NCC is a professor in the Department of Counseling and Education Psychology in the School of Education at Indiana University. He was director of the Center for Human Growth, a campus–community counseling center that serves as a training center for the Indiana University Department of Counseling and Educational Psychology from 1976 to 1992.

Thomas J. Sweeney, PhD, NCC, LPCC is a professor emeritus at Ohio University in Athens and special assistant to the dean of the School of Education at the University of North Carolina at Greensboro. He was the first chair of CACREP and served from 1981 to 1987. He is a past president of ACES as well as ACA (then APGA).

Richard A. Wantz, EdD, NCC is an associate professor and director of the Office for Counseling and Life Planning Services (OCLPS) in the Department of Human Services, College of Education and Human Services, at Wright State University in Dayton, Ohio.

John D. West, EdD, LPCC is a professor in the Counseling and Human Development Services Program at Kent State University in Kent, Ohio. He has supervised students in the program's clinic for 4years.

Joe Wittmer, PhD, NCC is a distinguished service professor in the Department of Counselor Education at the University of Florida. He served as chairperson of the ACES Committee on Accreditation (1979–1981) and as CACREP's first executive director (1981–1987).

INTRODUCTION

CHAPTER 1

COUNSELOR EDUCATION LABORATORIES: LESSONS FROM THE LITERATURE

Jane E. Myers
Alfred W. Smith

The *Accreditation Procedures Manual and Application* published by the Council for Accreditation of Counseling and Related Educational Programs (CACREP; 1988, 1994) includes standards for clinical instruction (part C, section III), including laboratory experiences, practica, and internships completed within a student's program of studies. The 1988 standards specify that clinical instruction is "taken throughout a student's program" (p. 28). The 1994 standards describe these experiences as "the most critical experience elements in the program" (p. 53). Obviously, programs seeking accreditation have a mandate to provide appropriate clinical instruction.

The standards provide guidance concerning the nature of facilities, supervisors, and types of experiences. The section concerning facilities is especially relevant here because this chapter's focus is on the means by which supervised experiences are provided in an on-campus setting under the direct supervision of counselor education program faculty. Presumably, all counselor education programs seeking accreditation will have or plan to have facilities for on-campus training because the 1988 standards specify that:

> Facilities for individual and/or group prepracticum and practicum experiences are available in a coordinated counseling laboratory setting

which is conducive to modeling and demonstration. It is under the direct control of the institution's academic unit in which the program is housed and includes but is not limited to the following....
(p. 28)

A review of these standards, which are included in the appendices to this monograph (along with the related glossary that defines the laboratory and practicum experiences), reveals a mandate to counselor education programs seeking accreditation to provide appropriate clinical instruction. Therefore, one might assume that the literature in counseling and counselor education would include a more or less voluminous body of data relative to counseling-training clinics. Unfortunately, this is not the case.

For example, a perusal of the Hollis and Wantz (1990) directory of counselor education training programs provides little information concerning the availability or nature of counseling laboratory training facilities. (Since this manuscript was written, Hollis and Wantz have modified their survey instrument so that future editions of their directory will contain data relative to on-campus clinics.) A recent study of curricular experiences in CACREP-accredited community counseling programs failed to provide data relative to clinical aspects of counselor training (Cowger, Hinkle, DeRidder, & Erk, 1991). In fact, the authors of this study did not mention or include clinical training in their survey.

As a result of an assignment to direct an ongoing clinical-training laboratory, the authors decided to seek information relative to similar operations in CACREP-accredited as well as nonaccredited programs. When the senior researcher presented the situation to other "clinic directors," a variety of remarks ensued. Some of the more notable and printable responses included:

- "You don't want to be a director if you're an assistant professor—it's a surefire way to never get tenure."
- "It's a way to have two full-time jobs with only one full-time salary."
- "I'm sorry for you. Good luck!"
- "You don't have release time for it? Oh boy!"

Because we were only able to obtain anecdotal information through these direct contacts, a literature search was conducted to ascertain the "state of the art" relative to counselor-training laboratories. It quickly became obvious that the overwhelming majority of available literature referred to psychology-training clinics, and that a paucity of literature exists relative to the operation of similar facilities within counselor preparation programs. Attempts to access the relevant literature in preparation for this chapter included personal contact with the librarians at both the American Counseling Association (ACA) and the American Psychological Association (APA) headquarters and computer searches of the PsychLIT and ERIC/CAPS databases. The keywords *counseling, counselor education, psychology,* and *marriage and family* were paired separately for each database search with each of the following keywords: *clinics, training clinics, clinical training, laboratories, accreditation, standards, practicum, internship, supervision, legal, ethical,* and *ethics.* The majority of citations that were identified through use of these keyword pairings reflected theoretical models and approaches to supervision, whereas there was a relative paucity of literature available that addressed trends and developments in on-campus clinical training. Psychology clinics were clearly predominant in the literature, with no citations found that discussed training clinics in counselor education or marriage and family programs.

This chapter provides a summary of the limited data available concerning psychology-training clinics. It begins with an overview of training clinics based in departments of psychology and the clinical-training issues identified in those clinics. Although the authors would greatly prefer to review and discuss counselor education clinics, the absence of available published literature prior to this book precludes that possibility. (A perusal of the remaining chapters of this book leads the reader to conclude that the situation described here is changing rapidly, fortunately.) Instead, we review the status of training clinics in a related profession, psychology, to determine lessons for counselor education programs in the development and implementation of our own clinical facilities. Implications for counselor education and accreditation of counselor-training clinic facilities are discussed in this chapter.

Overview of Psychology-Training Clinics

According to APA, there are 648 masters and doctoral preparation programs in psychology in the United States; most of them do not have clinical-training facilities, but they require clinical internships in a variety of settings. There are 438 APA-accredited internships in professional sites, usually other than university-based facilities (American Psychological Association, personal communication, May 4, 1992). Within the structure of the APA is an organization entitled The Association of Directors of Psychology Training Clinics (ADPTC). The ADPTC meets annually during the APA convention. Dues are $15 per year, for which members receive a newsletter and the opportunity to network with other members within the state, region, and national structure of APA. In 1989, the ADPTC included more than 120 members, including some counselor educators directing clinics in APA-accredited counseling psychology-training programs.

The ADPTC sponsored a symposium during the APA convention in 1989 entitled "The Training Clinic: Evolving Issues." Three papers were presented that addressed the areas of professional issues and ethics (Hailey, 1989), legal issues (Parvin, 1989), and models of training clinics in graduate psychology programs (Spruill, 1989). Spruill provided a summary of surveys conducted in 1983 and 1988 that identified the following trends in psychology clinics:

1. Clinic directors and directors of clinical training are not necessarily the same persons, nor do they enjoy the same status within psychology-training programs.
2. Most directors view clinical training as the primary function of psychology clinics (as opposed to services or research), with such training being provided in the context of clinical mental health care.
3. Providing service to the community was the second most important function of clinics, followed by research.
4. Most clinics operate 12 months a year and serve both the university and the community.
5. An emerging trend is having directors who are on nontenure tracks.

Spruill summarized the data as reflecting a diversity of models of training clinics. However, the issues being addressed within those clinics reflect a high degree of consistency.

Issues in Training Clinics: Contributions from Psychology

The major issues that emerge in the literature relative to training clinics may be summarized in terms of five major areas: (a) purpose of the clinic, (b) professional responsibility, (c) legal and ethical issues, (d) funding and evaluation issues, and (e) supervision.

Purpose of the Clinic

The purpose of the training clinic needs to be clarified because professional and ethical issues arise due to the special nature of clinics that are part of training programs. The most significant question to be answered is whether the primary purpose is training or service (Hailey, 1989), or research. This question is especially significant when community clients are seen in the clinic. One of the first issues to be considered when establishing an on-campus clinic is what to do with clients during term breaks. If the clinic operates according to the academic calendar, facilities may be locked or utilities turned off when the university is closed. During semester breaks, students may be unavailable to see clients, and faculty may be unavailable for supervision. If community service is a priority, formal arrangements must be made with community mental health agencies regarding emergency services for clients. Further, clients must be informed of these procedures.

Professional Responsibility

The purpose of the clinic has implications for the types of clientele accepted, as do the qualifications and expertise of faculty supervisors and the expertise and training needs of students. Decisions regarding which clients to accept, how to handle waiting lists, and how to conduct intakes and screening must be made (Cross, 1989). Decisions regarding termination or referral also must be made, and they may be based on the needs of the client or the clinician in training (which may be in conflict), or some other basis (Hailey, 1989). Reassignment of clients may result from (a) completion of a treatment plan, (b) completion of a practicum or internship, (c) counselor–client incompatibility, or (d) some other reason (Robison, Hutchinson, Barrick, & Angela, 1986). Responsibility to the client becomes both a professional responsibility and an ethical issue, especially when training of students is considered to be the primary purpose rather than the delivery of mental health services.

The role of the intern in clinics needs to be clearly defined. Lichtenberg (1987) noted that direct provision of clinical services is emphasized, whereas other components of professional competence, such as research, need to be emphasized as well. Again, the primary purpose of the clinic is reflected in the nature of the internship experience.

The role of the director also needs to be clarified. Often the director is responsible for overall clinic operation, but other faculty engage in supervision. The director may have little or no control over those faculty or the setting of policies to guide client service and/or supervision. This could include documentation of client service through case notes, documentation of supervision, and related issues that can affect the legal liability of the director (Cross, 1989; Hailey, 1989). Unfortunately, university politics and the academic rank-hath-its-privileges system may mitigate against the development of policies that protect the clients, the students, and/or the (clinic) faculty involved. Priorities assigned to clinical work, research, and coursework may place the director in conflict with departmental faculty.

Legal and Ethical Issues

Clinics operated in publicly funded institutions that serve the community face ethical dilemmas related to the provision of services when services conflict with priorities for training, clinic policies, or university schedules. The question of whether clinics can refuse to serve clients whose needs do not fit their training priorities is relevant. When fees are charged to clients, the determination of free services for clients participating in research needs to be made. If services are requested after the termination of the research, the responsibility for free services, supervision, automatic acceptance of the client, and related issues surface (Hailey, 1989).

Insurance payments can lead to additional legal and ethical issues, particularly if supervisors sign off for work performed by students. Such sign-offs may be viewed by third-party payers as insurance fraud (Cross, 1989; Hailey, 1989). Insurance for faculty and students working in clinics clearly is essential because litigation is always possible. The availability of supervision may be inadequate for such sign-offs, particularly when supervisory sessions are not documented. Such documentation could protect both the supervisor and the supervisee. Because the university may be liable when clinical services are provided, professional and legal criteria for services must be closely monitored (Parvin, 1989).

Parvin emphasized that training clinics provide modeling for students of professional mental health care. Therefore, it is important to have clinic policies reviewed by an attorney, as well as operating procedures such as case record keeping. Although extensive case notes may be helpful in student supervision, such notes could prove harmful to a client if subpoenaed for court purposes (Hailey, 1989). Protection of confidentiality needs to be clearly specified in the operating procedures of the clinic. In addition, procedures for handling potentially dangerous or suicidal clients need to be written and clear. Some attorneys have recommended that a licensed psychologist be present and available at all times when clients are seen in the clinic (Cross, 1989).

Funding and Evaluation Issues

The availability of federal funding for clinical psychology training is an important resource for students. At the same time, the guidelines mandated by funding sources may conflict with the requirements of APA for program accreditation (Strickland & Calkins, 1987). Outside funding is increasingly sought by clinics because they are increasingly expected to generate all or some of their budgetary needs. Fees for client services contribute to the support of the clinic. Spruill (1989) noted that these fees vary between $0 and $100 per hour, although the modal and median figures are both $5 per hour at the time of this writing. There is tremendous variability among clinics regarding the disbursement of fees collected.

Edelstein (1985) noted that there is a lack of published data concerning the identification and validation of competencies and outcome goals for graduate students, including those seeing clients in a university clinic. This is due, in part, to the lack of uniform evaluation activities within clinical-training programs. Edelstein recommended the development of a standardized means of evaluating competencies desired to be developed through training clinics. In addition to clinical-treatment skills, these would include skills in assessment, research, and teaching. Obstacles to evaluation include: (a) resource constraints, (b) staff resistance, (c) technological limitations, and (d) need for better outcome measures (Stevenson & Norcross, 1985).

Supervision

The division of supervisory responsibility in clinic facilities is an important issue (Cross, 1989). For example, is the director to provide coverage for absent faculty supervisors? It is common for directors to complain that faculty, department chairs, and deans provide little support for their needs. Clinic directors are often unable to set policies that are followed by supervising faculty, many of whom are part time or volunteers (Spruill, 1989). Further, because the trend is to have nontenure-track faculty serve as directors, their ability to influence departmental policies is limited.

Although most supervisors have release time equivalent to one course, the demands of the job create excessive commitments of their time. Hailey

(1989) noted that most psychology clinic directors report feeling over-whelmed.

Summary

Several points may be made concerning the literature reviewed here as it relates to the field of psychology. First, it is clear that psychologists have been grappling with issues related to training clinics for many years. Second, APA has responded to the needs of clinic staff through: (a) the formation of a network, (b) the development and ongoing revision of national directories, and (c) the development of national standards for accreditation of clinic facilities that provide internship opportunities. Third, psychology clinic directors have identified a number of critical issues facing clinical training programs. Fourth, accountability, evaluation, and the identification of clinical competencies are areas in need of development. Clinical training within counselor education programs has received far less attention in the professional literature. In fact, with the exception of the CACREP standards, which mandate a "coordinated counseling laboratory setting" for programs seeking accreditation, there is a virtual dearth of information in the counseling literature pertaining to counselor education clinics.

Based on similarities in clinical training across settings, it seems safe to assume that counselor education programs operating clinical-training facilities will encounter at least the variety and type of issues identified by psychologists in relation to psychology-training clinics. It also seems safe to assume that additional issues unique to counselor preparation will emerge as we study our own clinical-training facilities and programs. The role of the clinical-training director is and will continue to be an important one. The current system of learning how to be a director is a word-of-mouth mentoring activity, assuming a newly assigned director such as the senior author knows other counselor educators who serve as clinic directors. Counselor education programs wanting to establish clinics must learn from psychology and through personal contact. Our literature base is clearly lacking, as are training opportunities relevant to the specific needs of clinical-training directors. Numerous other issues, such as those identified in this chapter, will be equally as important in the future.

Clearly, both dialogue and research regarding counselor education training clinics are not only needed but are long overdue. As a profession, we have *somewhat* neglected an integral part of our training programs. The somewhat is emphasized because many (and no one now knows just how many) counselor education programs have an on-campus laboratory or clinic operating in any of a number of ways. Examples are provided in almost every chapter of this book. Counselor educators need to share information and ideas, and should begin to dialogue concerning clinical training and supervision of counselors. Some steps in this direction are now underway.

In January 1992, the ACES Interest Network for Directors of Clinical Training and Clinics (DCTC) was formed. The first meeting of the Network occurred during the AACD convention in Baltimore in March 1992. A direct outcome of this meeting was a 7-hour think-tank program at the national ACES convention in the fall of 1992, the proceedings of which comprise this book. Joe Hollis and Richard Wantz were involved in the ACES program and the DCTC and agreed to include questions related to the availability of clinic facilities and programs in the next issue of their comprehensive directory (see Hollis & Wantz, 1990). The network will continue to meet at each national ACA and ACES convention. In addition, ACES funded a small research project in 1992 to study counselor education training clinics. These initial steps may make only a small dent in our need for knowledge of counselor-training clinics, but they do signify that a somewhat neglected area in counselor training is now receiving attention. The cumulative effect of recent changes ultimately will help to improve clinical training for all counselors.

Implications

1. The role of the director of a counselor education training laboratory needs to be clarified. The demands of this position relative to the needs of the department and the requirements of faculty for promotion and tenure need to be examined. It seems that clinic directors may be caught in a double bind: Their services are needed or even required by departments, yet the time commitment required and the services provided do not fit the academic reward system.
2. Some type of training or orientation for the role of director needs to be developed. The current word-of-mouth mentoring system is inadequate to prepare competent clinic directors in a relatively short period of time.

3. Research is needed concerning all aspects of clinic operation, including the relative value of on-campus versus off-campus sites for supervised clinical instruction.
4. ACES needs to continue to encourage dialogue among counselor educators concerning on-campus clinical training.
5. The CACREP standards for clinical training need to be examined and possibly revised to reflect current exemplary practices and research findings.
6. Policies, procedures, and guidelines for operating clinics need to be developed and disseminated to counselor education programs. As it currently stands, many counselor education departments wanting to establish or improve their clinics are in the position of reinventing the wheel, rather than learning from the experiences, mistakes, and successes of their peers.

References

Council for Accreditation of Counseling and Related Educational Programs. (1988). *Accreditation procedures manual.* Alexandria, VA: Author.

Council for Accreditation of Counseling and Related Educational Programs. (1994). *CACREP accreditation standards and procedures manual.* Alexandria, VA: Author.

Cowger, E.L., Hinkle, J.S., DeRidder, L.M., & Erk, R. (1991). CACREP community counseling programs: Present status and implications for the future. *Journal of Mental Health Counseling, 13*(2), 172–186.

Cross, H. (1989). *The Association of Directors of Psychology Training Clinics, Newsletter #21.* Yakima, WA: Seattle State University Press.

Edelstein, B.A. (1985). Empirical evaluation of clinical training. *Behavior Therapist, 8*(4), 67–70.

Hailey, B.J. (1989, August). *The training clinic evolving issues: Professional issues and ethics.* Paper presented at the annual convention of the American Psychological Association, New Orleans, LA.

Hollis, J., & Wantz, R. (1990). *Counselor preparation 1990–93.* Muncie, IN: Accelerated Development.

Lichtenberg, J.W. (1987). A missing component in most internships. *Counseling Psychologist, 15*(2), 267–270.

Parvin, J.D. (1989, August). *The training clinic evolving issues: Legal issues in the training clinic.* Paper presented at the annual convention of the American Psychological Association, New Orleans, LA.

Robison, F.F., Hutchinson, R.L., Barrick, A.L., & Angela, N. (1986). Reassigning clients: Practices used by counseling centers. *Journal of Counseling Psychology, 33*(4), 465–468.

Spruill, J. (1989, August). *The training clinic evolving issues: Models of training clinics in graduate psychology programs.* Paper presented at the American Psychological Association, New Orleans, LA.

Stevenson, J.F., & Norcross, J.C. (1985). Evaluation activity in psychology training clinics: National survey findings. *Professional Psychology Research Practice, 16*(1), 29–41.

Strickland, B.R., & Calkins, B.J. (1987). Public policy and clinical training. *Clinical Psychologist, 40*(2), 31–34.

PART I

THE CACREP STANDARDS FOR COUNSELOR EDUCATION LABORATORIES

CHAPTER 2

EVOLUTION OF THE CACREP STANDARDS

Joe Wittmer

The late Dr. Robert O. Stripling, known affectionately within the counseling profession as the "Father of Counselor Preparation Standards," left his entire set of papers regarding the evolution of the Council for the Accreditation of Counseling and Related Educational Programs (CACREP) training standards to my care. Among dozens of pages of memos, letters, rough drafts, and so on, one 8-page, handwritten document dated January 9, 1959, stands out: the first (in the opinion of the writer) draft ever written of what has now become known as the CACREP standards. The purpose of this chapter is to provide an overview of the contents of these standards relative to counseling laboratory facilities and training, and to review the evolution of this particular section of the standards from 1959 to the present.

Standards for On-Campus Clinics: 1959–1963

Amazingly, the core aspects of the standards of counselor preparation have not changed substantially from Dr. Stripling's original draft. However, his first draft concerned only standards for preparing secondary school counselors. The handwritten document referred to previously contained a description of supervised practice, which included practicum, internship, and the on-campus clinic (laboratory). Concerning the latter, Stripling wrote:

> One essential aspect of counselor preparation is supervised practice in counseling and related guidance activities. Such practice, planned

in appropriate settings, both off and on the campus, includes observation and working directly with secondary school age youth. It also includes professional relationships with school counselors and personnel in related pupil personnel services as well as with other members of the school staff, community agency personnel and parents.

I. Three Aspects of Supervised Practice:

A. Laboratory experiences may be self contained or integrated with classroom instruction. They involve both observation of and participation in activities relating to the total guidance program such as analyzing case records, testing and test interpretation, role playing in counseling and group work, observing demonstrations, and working with guidance materials. Laboratory experiences appropriate to the counselor candidates' needs should be a part of the entire counselor education program. (Stripling, 1959)

As noted, the standards related to the "clinic" written in 1959 remain relatively similar to the description in the current CACREP manual being used in accreditation of counselor education programs (Council for the Accreditation of Counseling and Related Educational Programs, 1988, 1991). Obviously, the clinic facilities, recording equipment, and so on have improved drastically since 1959.

Dr. Stripling's notes indicate that, in 1959, he was asked to chair the soon-to-be developed Association of Counselor Educators and Supervisors (ACES) National Committee on Counselor Education Standards in the Preparation of Secondary School Counselors. Other members of that first ACES Standards Committee, appointed by ACES on May 16, 1960, included the following ACES regional chairpersons: (a) Western —Earl F. Carnes; (b) Rocky Mountain—Lyle L. Miller; (c) North Central—Emery G. Kennedy; (d) North Atlantic —Henry L. Isaksen; and (e) Southern— Merritt C. Oelke.

Additionally, Dr. Stripling's notes indicate that there were six at-large members: (a) Harold F. Cottingham, (b) Lowell Bell, (c) Willis E. Dugan, (d) Bruce E. Shear, (e) Harry Smallenburg, and (f) H. Edgar Williams.

This committee (which, according to Dr. Stripling's notes, shortened its name to the National Committee on Counselor Education Standards during its second year of existence) adopted the following schedule for its 4-year cooperative study of counselor education standards:

- 1960–1961: Regional study groups organized and working
- 1961: American Personnel and Guidance Association (APGA) convention: Progress report at the business meeting

- 1961–1962: National Association of Guidance Supervisors and Counselor Trainers (NAGSCT) regional meetings devoted to cooperative study
- 1962: APGA convention: Program on Cooperative Study 1962–1963: (1) intensive study of various areas at both regional and national levels; and (2) regional and institutional implementation
- 1963: APGA convention: Progress report on implementation
- 1963–1964: Development of final report
- 1964: APGA convention: Final report

During the period of the study (1960–1964) noted previously, approximately 1,000 professional persons associated with counselor education, counselor supervision, and counseling and guidance practices in secondary schools, as well as other school, government, and professional association personnel, contributed to the study. The ACES Standards Committee completed its agenda as scheduled; ACES adopted the standards during the 1964 APGA convention in San Francisco.

On January 28, 1962, Dr. Stripling sent the first *Working Paper on Standards for Counselor Education in the Preparation of Secondary School Counselors* to his committee members for their individual comments. The "laboratory" (clinic) section had changed somewhat since the first draft in 1959. The 1962 "working paper" description was as follows:

> Three aspects of supervised experience are recognized in the counselor education program; laboratory experiences, practicum experiences and internship.
>
> a. laboratory experiences are provided during the first year.
>
> 1) Opportunities are provided for both observation and participation in activities related to the total guidance program, e.g., role-playing, listening to tapes, testing, organizing and using pupil personnel records, working with professional personnel, preparing and examining case studies, and using educational and occupational information materials.
>
> 2) Laboratory experiences appropriate to the counselor candidate's needs are a continuing part of the counselor education program.
>
> 3) Plans and procedures adopted by the staff clearly describe the integration of such experiences. (Stripling, 1962)

The comments on the "working paper" (written on the margins) by the national committee (except for one member who did not comment) were returned to Dr. Stripling. He compiled their comments and produced another draft of the standards during 1963. Only a word or two changed in the 1963 "clinic" description as given previously.

Development of the Standards: 1964–1979

The American School Counselor Association (ASCA) teamed up with ACES in the early 1960s and two massive studies were conducted regarding the standards. In 1964, ACES adopted the standards and published the Counselor Preparation Opinionaire, followed by 3 more years of study and use on a trial basis (ACES, 1964). Then, in 1967, the first *Manual for Self-Study by a Counselor Education Staff* was produced by ACES in co-operation with ASCA (ACES, 1967). The former was written by James Grubb and the latter by George Hill, both from the Ohio University. Grubb's 1964 80-item Counselor Preparation Opinionaire covered all aspects of the then (recently) adopted ACES standards for training secondary school counselors. The opinionaire was written in a manner that permitted counselor education faculty to check their specific preparation program against the standards and yielded a total raw score, with 5 points being the highest score possible for each of the 80 items. Four items, numbers 27–30, on the opinionaire queried individual counselor education faculty regarding the on-campus laboratory (the word *clinic* did not appear in the CACREP manual until 1987) as follows:

27. The facilities are equipped with recording and listening devices for observation and supervision.
28. One-way vision screens are located in such a way as to provide for observation by an individual or a whole class.
29. Conference rooms are provided for tape analysis and small group conferences.
30. Portable records (tape recorders) are available in sufficient number.

Each of the 80 items on Grubb's 1964 opinionaire was followed by a 1–5 Likert scale response choice, with the scale ranging from "not available" to "completely adequate."

In addition to these 1967 standards, the Standards for Preparation of Elementary School Counselors were written in 1968. Subsequently, in

1969, the Guidelines for Graduate Programs in the Preparation of Student Personnel Workers in Higher Education were developed. In 1973, these three sets of standards were rewritten and combined into the Standards for the Preparation of Counselors and Other Personnel Services Specialists. The latter standards were adopted by ACES in 1973, by ASCA in 1977, and by APGA in 1977. Also approved by ACES in 1977 were the Guidelines for Doctoral Preparation in Counselor Education (Altekruse & Wittmer, 1991).

None of the previously mentioned standards were used for official accreditation decisions until 1979, with the exception of a variation used for state approval in the state of Wisconsin (1972) and state accreditation by California ACES during 1973 (Altekruse & Wittmer, 1991). During 1979, the standards were used by the ACES National Committee on Accreditation to accredit four counselor education programs on a pilot basis. Only minor changes in the overall standards were made by the ACES committee between 1977 and 1979, and no changes were made in the "laboratory" clinic standards.

As noted, the clinic standards changed very little (except for being shortened significantly) between 1963 and 1979 when published by APGA. The 1979 APGA publication stated that:

> a) Laboratory experiences, providing both observation and participation in specific activities, are offered throughout the preparatory program. This might include role playing, listening to tapes, viewing videotape playbacks, testing, organizing and using personnel records, interviews with field practitioners, preparing and examining case studies, and using career information materials. (American Personnel and Guidance Association, 1979, p. 8)

CACREP Standards: 1980–1988

In 1980, the ACES Committee on Accreditation (the writer was chairperson of this committee) agreed to accept all of California's ACES (CACES) previous accreditation decisions (five programs), provided CACES ceased accrediting counselor preparation programs. This left ACES as the only association accrediting body using the standards of training. In 1981, the APGA board of directors adopted a resolution to gain control over the responsibilities of the ACES accrediting body. With this action, CACREP was officially formed as an independent accrediting body sponsored by APGA and several participating divisions. CACREP accepted all counselor-preparation programs previously accreditated by ACES (including those by CACES).

CACREP adopted the existing standards at its first meeting in September 1981. Although the first few years of CACREP brought about many suggested changes in the preparation standards, the 1981–1985 CACREP standards reveal the exact wording for describing the on-campus laboratory as taken from the 1979 APGA document noted earlier. The first major changes since the inception of the standards were introduced by CACREP in 1986. The "new" revised standards became the official standards of CACREP on July 1, 1988; except for some minor changes made by CACREP during 1991 (most 1991 changes concerned CACREP specialties), the current standards will remain in effect until July 1, 1994 (Altekruse & Wittmer, 1991).

Writers of the 1988 CACREP standards revised the description of the clinic and described the "laboratory" experience and related standards under Section III: Clinical Instruction. As noted, this is the first time the term *clinical instruction* appeared in the CACREP standards (Council for the Accreditation of Counseling and Related Educational Programs, 1988). Also noted, CACREP did a brief revision in the 1988 standards during 1991. However, again, the wording describing the laboratory remains similiar to the 1988 CACREP standards (Council for the Accreditation of Counceling and Related Educational Programs, 1991). The 1988 CACREP description of the on-campus clinic is as follows:

> D. Facilities for supervised individual and/or group prepracticum and practicum experiences are available in a coordinated counseling laboratory setting which is conductive to modeling and demonstration. It is under the direct control of the institution's academic unit in which the program is housed and includes, but is not limited to the following:
>
> 1. individual counseling rooms, with assured privacy and sufficient space for appropriate equipment (e.g., videotape and audiotape).
> 2. rooms for small group work, with assured privacy and sufficient space for appropriate equipment.
> 3. portable and permanent audio- and videotape recording, and playing equipment.
> 4. rooms with one-way vision glass.
> 5. acoustical (i.e. sound reduction) treatment throughout.
> 6. exemplary, current professional resources including career, leisure, and occupational information materials, standardized tests and interpretation aids, and microcomputer equipment.

E. Technical assistance for the use and maintenance of audio and videotape, and microcomputer equipment is available. (Council for the Accreditation of Counseling and Related Educational Programs, 1988, p. 28)

On-Campus Standards: 1994

In October 1992, CACREP approved a new set of standards to go into effect July 1, 1994, and to remain in effect for 7 years (Council for the Accreditation of Counseling and Related Educational Programs, 1993). The 1994 CACREP standards concerning the clinic are identical to the 1988 and 1991 standards.

Summary and Conclusions

In light of the dramatic changes in our profession during the past 30 years, it is interesting that the counselor preparation standards relating to the on-campus clinic have changed very little since first published by the ACES Committee (chaired by Dr. Robert Stripling) in its 1962 working paper. As a matter of fact, the description of the clinic has not changed significantly from Dr. Stripling's 1959 handwritten description. However, what has changed (in this writer's opinion) is the *original intent* of the clinic's role in counselor preparation. From my long-time personal and professional relationship with Dr. Stripling, I know that his idea of the on-campus clinic was that of a facility to be used in prepracticum experiences only (role-playing, etc.), as opposed to practicum or internship experiences. That is, the original ACES standards clearly recognized three separate, exclusive, stand-alone, supervised experiences: (a) prepracticum laboratory, (b) practicum, and (c) internship. Dr. Stripling's notes revealed, "The laboratory experiences should adequately prepare students for the in-the-field practica" (Stripling, 1959). It should be acknowledged that the institution where Dr. Stripling worked as a counselor educator (University of Florida, 1941–1980) has always (and continues to this date) utilized the on-campus clinic as a prepracticum facility as opposed to a practicum site. It can be observed in this chapter that the term *practicum experiences* did not appear in the clinic description until the 1988 CACREP revision (those being used today).

It is this writer's belief that the CACREP standards, as now written, do not adequately cover "good standards of practice" for use of the clinic as

23

an on-campus practicum site. This lack of emphasis on the other than "facility" aspects of the clinic (within the CACREP standards) is directly related to the confusion concerning its use as intended by the original ACES/CACREP standards writers. According to this writer's review, the on-campus laboratory was never intended as a practicum experience site, yet laboratories today are commonly used for both practicum and internship experiences, as well as prepracticum training in basic helping skills.

Implications and Recommendations

My experiences in sorting through Dr. Stripling's historical papers have led me to believe that ACA should develop an archive for the profession. Now is the time. Such historical papers tend to get lost if not appropriately cataloged and stored. In addition to this need, the following implications are relevant for the profession.

1. If the on-campus counseling laboratory is to be used as a practicum site (i.e., with "real-life" clients), the CACREP standards should clearly address both the "physical facility" and the "counseling clinic" (i.e., standards concerning client welfare, ethical and legal aspects of the on-campus clinic, etc.). Current CACREP standards (and the forthcoming 1994 ones) address only the former and are inadequate if the clinic is going to be used for practicum experiences (as such experiences are described in the current CACREP standards).

2. It appears obvious to this writer that it is the contention of many, if not most counselor educators, that the on-campus practicum is superior to the off-campus experience. However, where is the research to support this contention? If current, modern equipment is effectively utilized by the off-campus practicum site hosts (video recordings for use by faculty supervisors on campus, etc.), is the on-campus clinic really the superior method of training? Perhaps an ACES committee or more ACES think tanks should be appointed to address this important issue.

3 It appears obvious that the CACREP standards concerning the use of the clinic as an on-campus practicum (with real clients) are inadequate. Thus, if counselor education programs plan to continue using the clinic as a practicum experience, the CACREP standards need immediate attention.

References

Altekruse, M., & Wittmer, J. (1991). Accreditation in counselor education. In F. Bradley (Ed.), *Credentialing in counseling* (pp. 53–63). Alexandria, VA: American Counseling Association.

Asociation of Counselor Educators and Supervisors. (1964). Standards for counselor education in the preparation of secondary school counselors. *Personnel and Guidance Journal, 42,* 1060–1073.

Asociation of Counselor Educators and Supervisors. (1967). *Manual for self study by a counselor education staff.* Washington, DC: Author.

American Personnel and Guidance Association. (1979). *Standards for preparation in counselor education.* Washington, DC: Author.

Council for the Accreditation of Counseling and Related Educational Programs. (1988). *Accreditation procedures manual and application.* Alexandria, VA: Author.

Council for the Accreditation of Counseling and Related Educational Programs. (1991). *Accreditation procedures manual and application.* Alexandria, VA: Author.

Council for the Accreditation of Counseling and Related Educational Programs. (1993). *Accreditation procedures manual and application.* Alexandria, VA: Author.

Stripling, R. O. (1959). *Counselor preparation standards: A draft. Handwritten notes.* Gainesville, FL: University of Florida Press.

Stripling, R. O. (1962). *Working paper on standards for counselor education in the preparation of secondary school counselors.* Unpublished manuscript, University of Florida, Gainesville, FL.

CHAPTER 3

UNDERSTANDING THE CACREP CLINICAL STANDARDS

Carol L. Bobby
Joseph R. Kandor

Since the initial publication of standards for preparation in counselor education, there has been a continued expectation that supervised experiences be provided to students within preparation programs. These standards, as adopted and periodically revised by the Council for Accreditation of Counseling and Related Educational Programs (CACREP), have also required that programs provide laboratory facilities for modeling and demonstration purposes. A review of both the historical and present standards in the context of benefits of, as well as inhibitors to, creating separate clinics within counselor education departments is provided in this chapter.

Historical Development of the CACREP Standards

In 1979, the American Personnel and Guidance Association (APGA), now the American Counseling Association (ACA), published a historical document for the Association for Counselor Education and Supervision (ACES) entitled *Standards for Preparation in Counselor Education* (American Personnel and Guidance Association, 1979). This booklet contained standards for entry preparation (master's and specialist degree programs), advanced preparation (doctoral degree programs), and specific program areas (school counselor and other personnel services specialists). It represented the culmination of over 20 years of discussions, drafts of standards, feasibility research, publications, and collaboration among practitioners and counselor educators interested in providing guidelines for the evaluation of existing or the establishment of new counselor preparation programs. Using this publication, programs interested in accountability could assess themselves against a set of minimum criteria considered necessary for appropriate preparation of counseling professionals.

In 1981, CACREP was incorporated as an independent organization for the purpose of monitoring, revising, and implementing the Standards for Preparation in Counselor Education. Its board of directors, representing ACA and participating divisions, was charged with (a) promoting the standards, (b) assisting with their implementation, (c) reviewing programs seeking to be accredited under the standards, (d) developing avenues of cooperation among programs of preparation and practicing professionals, and (e) working with other accrediting associations in promoting quality education for counselors and student-affairs practitioners.

Standards for Clinical Instruction

A review of the standards throughout their history, with specific regard given to clinical instruction, reveals a continued expectation for supervised experiences to be offered within the preparation program. In addition, the standards have required that "facilities" be provided in a "coordinated laboratory setting." The wording of the *facilities-related* standards has changed only slightly throughout the years, yet the changes provide potential insight into CACREP's expectations for counselor education laboratories/clinics. The exact wording of the standards and their subsequent revisions appear next.

> *Pre-1988 Standards, Standard IV.10.b:* Facilities for supervised experiences are provided in a coordinated laboratory setting on campus. (American Personnel and Guidance Association, 1979, p. 16)
>
> *July 1988 Standards, Standard III.D:* Facilities for supervised individual and/or group prepracticum and practicum experiences are available in a coordinated counseling laboratory setting which is conducive to modeling and demonstration. It is under the direct control of the institution's academic unit in which the program is housed. (Council for Accreditation of Counseling and Related Educational Programs, 1988, p. 28)

January 1994 Standards, Standard III.D: A counseling laboratory that is conducive to modeling, demonstration, and training is available and used for clinical instruction. Administrative control of the laboratory facility allows adequate and appropriate access by the program. (Council for Accreditation of Counseling and Related Educational Programs, 1994, p. 53)

It is noted that the original (pre-1988) standards required only that facilities be provided "on campus." In 1988, the standards required facilities "under the direct control of the institution's academic unit," with the academic unit meaning the counselor education department. The 1988 standards further outlined that the supervised experiences included prepracticum and practicum experiences.

The 1994 CACREP Standards

In 1994, the CACREP board will require that a laboratory with "adequate and appropriate access" be available to accredited program(s). Hence, an in-house clinical facility is not necessary, but programs must demonstrate that their students have time and space available in a counseling laboratory.

The return to a less prescriptive facilities requirement in the 1994 standards reflects the CACREP board's recognition that: (a) many programs have never been able to offer in-house clinical facilities, but have been able to demonstrate access to appropriate facilities; (b) higher education fiscal restraints and cutbacks are continuing to grow; (c) the standards are minimum requirements for quality preparation; and (d) the majority of students' clinical hours are to be completed during internship, typically off-campus or "out in the field," which raises issues of cost-effectiveness for requiring departmental clinics for prepracticum and practicum hours. At the minimum, CACREP still requires access to laboratories for "modeling, demonstration, and training," which may or may not be different than full-service clinics providing counseling services to diverse populations with a variety of presenting problems.

Benefits of and Inhibitors to On-Campus Clinics

Although the CACREP standards do not necessitate that a program-operated clinic be established, there are many attractive benefits to such an option. Such benefits include: (a) the ability for more direct observation of students' skills through observation and live supervision, (b) the ability for faculty to maintain and further hone their own counseling skills, (c) the capacity to more easily research the effectiveness of counseling models and techniques, and (d) the ability to develop new avenues of service to the community.

There are also major inhibitors to program-operated clinics. Financial inhibitors include the cost of developing the clinic facility, staffing with both professionals and support personnel, insurance, equipment maintenance, marketing, and other general operating expenses. Such financial considerations are amplified in light of the current fiscal crisis felt by most institutions of higher education. The development of program-based clinics also requires consideration of legal and ethical issues such as the liability incurred by having potentially low skill level or entering practicum students make diagnoses and provide services to the population at large. Ethical issues are raised through record-keeping requirements, clinical research, and taping or observation requirements. If CACREP standards were to require full-service clinics, it is probable that a call for more elaborate clinical facility accreditation standards would be necessitated.

Conclusion

In conclusion, the dialogue on clinical facilities with regard to the requirements of the CACREP standards is important and should continue. The history of the standards documents a commitment to the concept of facilities for modeling and training purposes. The standards also document a continuing commitment to supervision, taping and observation capabilities, and field experience with "individuals and groups within the appropriate work setting" (Association for Counselor Education and Supervision, Standards for Preparation II.C.1(b), 1979, p. 22) or "clientele appropriate to the program emphasis" (Council for Accreditation of Counseling and Related Educational Programs, Standards III.H.1 and III.I.1, 1988, pp. 28–29). To date, some CACREP-accredited programs offer full-service clinics, whereas some simply document access to facilities. Both types of programs meet the "spirit" of the standards and, in the judgment of the CACREP board, offer quality preparation.

References

American Personnel and Guidance Association. (1979). *Standards for preparation in counselor education.* Falls Church, VA: Author.

Council for Accreditation of Counseling and Related Educational Programs. (1988). *Accreditation procedures manual and application.* Alexandria, VA: Author.

Council for Accreditation of Counseling and Related Educational Programs. (1994). *CACREP accreditation standards and procedures manual.* Alexandria, VA: Author.

CHAPTER 4

IMPLEMENTATION OF THE CACREP LABORATORY STANDARDS

Thomas J. Sweeney

The attention being focused on "laboratory" standards is unique. A review of the history of the language and length of this section of the Council for Accreditation of Counseling and Related Educational Programs (CACREP) standards reveals little change in three decades since their inception in the 1960s (see chapter 2). Not surprisingly, surveys of attitudes related to the importance or acceptance of the standards consistently address the requirements for supervised experiences, ratios of students to faculty, and related issues, but not the requirements for the laboratory itself (Bobby & Kandor, 1992; Vacc, 1992). Having (a) reviewed many accreditation applications, (b) visited a variety of large and small counselor education programs, (c) directed a counselor education guidance center for 8 years, and (d) maintained contact with colleagues around the country, this writer believes that there is a number of common inhibitors to fully meeting the spirit and letter of the CACREP standards for a laboratory facility. Why this section of the standards may be difficult to implement, and what benefits meeting them brings to a program, are addressed in the following sections under (a) inhibitors, (b) advantages, and (c) implications.

Inhibitors to Laboratory Standards Implementation

There has been a trend over the last decade or more for counselor education practica and internship experiences to be conducted in off-campus locations using on-site clinical supervisors rather than university faculty as supervisors (Hollis & Wantz, 1990). For example, although prepracticum laboratory experiences associated with basic helping relationships skills training may be conducted under faculty supervision, these experiences are often role-play situations and best suited to basic relationship development and structuring techniques. Given that off-campus practica are a relatively common practice, CACREP reviewers and the council have not perceived any deficiency among programs seeking accreditation that provide practica in this manner. When the standards were first drafted, however, school counseling was the major focus of counselor education, and even school counseling was very different than it is today. Counselor educators were often not experienced counselors. As a consequence, counselor education students were getting their most relevant experiences from supervisors in the field. One question for the future, then, concerns the adequacy of the laboratory standards; they were written 30 years ago and remain basically unchanged today despite obvious changes in counselor education and society.

Elsewhere in this book, the specific language of the 1988 and 1994 standards are detailed (see chapters 2 and 3 and appendices). In short, the standards specify that there shall be facilities for both individual- and group-supervised experiences "conducive to modeling, demonstration, and training." Likewise, they specify that there shall be "exemplary, current resources," "technical assistance for the use and maintenance of audio and videotape, and microcomputer equipment" (p. 28). These are no small requirements for any counselor education program.

However, an essential question concerns the purposes of the facilities. Are they principally for the purposes of students practicing prepracticum human-relations skills, viewing videotapes of "experts" or examining specimen appraisal sets or career resources? Although these illustrate some of the possible uses, they may not justify the substantial capital and personnel outlay to support such a facility. Even more germane, they may fall far short of the needs of the students today to experience close faculty supervision of their first efforts to practice counseling.

The challenge to counselor education programs to meet the CACREP standards requires attention to the purposes of clinical training, along with a number of inhibitors that, commonly experienced by counselor education programs, prevent them from fully meeting the CACREP standards. These inhibitors, listed and discussed next, must be addressed if counselor education programs are to meet or (with hope) exceed the stated purposes of clinics per the standards.

1. Realistic Client Contacts Commensurate with Counselor Trainee Competence

Elsewhere in the standards, reference is made to counselor trainees having experience with clients suited to their anticipated environmental setting. School, mental health, college, marriage and family, gerontological, and career counselors all might benefit from some experience with counselees different than their specializations. Some programs provide a prepracticum laboratory or practicum with college-age students in undergraduate classes. In most cases, counselor education programs tend to provide basic skills and theory for their students and expect the on-site facilities to provide the specialized client contact.

One inhibiting issue for an effort to do more relates to the trainees' level of competence and the reality of screening clients who can be limited to a quarter or semester system of service. Such contact also places the clinic in the dual role of training facility and mental health agency, as discussed by other authors in this book (e.g., chapters 10, 18, and 20). Even with the best of intentions, matching trainee competence with client needs is logistically and ethically challenging. However, without opportunities for such counselee contact, there may be little justification for the other inhibitors being overcome, such as space, technical assistance, and faculty time requirements.

2. Expense in Providing Suitable Clinical Supervision

The issue of expense is an inhibitor throughout the standards. However, clinical supervision is high on the list of every university administrator when budget considerations are at hand. The cost is compounded for the vast majority of programs that do not have doctoral students who need or can be assigned supervisory loads. If there is no "laboratory" or similar facility with actual counselee services provided, the added expense for intensive supervision can be minimized.

3. Liability Issues

The nature of our society today seems to be "sue now" and see who is right later. The legislative credentialing of counselors predictably has contributed to this inhibitor. With laws defining our practice comes a basis for "malpractice" and other such legal complications relatively new to the profession. It may be one of the prices for our success in gaining equity in the marketplace. However, even before the current concerns for liability of supervisors for trainee behavior, universities have never been eager to extend their institutional liability without adequate justification.

4. Ethical Issues

Client records, assessments, diagnoses, treatment plans, and referrals are subjects in a number of classes in the curriculum. In an actual clinical setting, provision for the appropriate recording, storing, and management of such data becomes critically important. The opportunity for ethical issues to surface increases as well. Care in the use of information, deliberate modeling of ethical decision making, and attention to overseeing the proper use of data all add to the load of the faculty, all of whom are already busy with other issues associated with carrying out the responsibilities of a counselor educator.

5. Maintaining a Facility

To establish a "laboratory" or clinical facility requires a concerted effort to acquire the space and have it suitably equipped. Having achieved that task, however, is less than half of the job. Keeping it equipped, comfortable, and attractive to the publics served becomes a continuing responsibility. The author recalls a broken window shade, which seemed to have been broken forever, on which some frustrated individual wrote in chalk, "fix me!" University finances were tight at best, and the message hung there much too long. When the author was a student, the "counseling office" was a cubicle with a table, two chairs, and what seemed like a huge two-way window. Today, microcomputers, their software, video and audio equipment, and any number of assessment instruments require updating, maintenance, and periodic replacement. All of this is in addition to consideration of the furniture, wall hangings, and like creature comforts so important to a public service facility.

6. Technical and Clerical Assistance

Someone must see to the operation of the day-to-day activities of the facility. Calls for information, appointments, cancellations, attention to records, billing (when appropriate), and a multitude of details related to the equipment, scheduling of rooms, and availability of counselors and supervisors are essential to the smooth operation of any facility. The absence of such personnel is clearly an inhibitor. Likewise, making provisions for such assistance is an inhibitor because it is a continuing cost that tends to increase with time.

7. Faculty and/or Someone's Time to Manage and Market Services

It is possible for an experienced doctoral assistant to handle some of the responsibilities for managing and marketing the counselor education counseling services. Nevertheless, a faculty or staff member must allocate time to help negotiate for-fee services with outside organizations, supervise intake interviews, and generally ensure the proper operation of the services and facility. In the case of programs without doctoral assistants, this inhibiting factor is even greater.

8. Lack of Incentives to Be Involved as Faculty

Discussions with some of the most successful and longest running facility personnel suggest that one person can make or break a clinic. The ideal is a person who enjoys and/or appreciates the value of such an assignment, accepts the position, and provides leadership. In the absence of such a person, there are few incentives for assuming this responsibility. In fact, release time, additional pay, and support services are necessary if there is to be a long-term commitment by any member of the faculty. Within the higher education reward system, (a) research, (b) publications, (c) grants, (d) leadership positions within the profession, and (e) other visible signs of professional and academic accomplishment are the symbols of collegial esteem needed for merit salary increments, promotion, and, more importantly, tenure. This is not to say that the work is not valued by some faculty or administrators. In general practice, however, this is perceived more as a "good citizen" type of responsibility than, say, the management of a research or training grant.

9. Ease with Which Off-Campus Placements "Solve" All the Other Inhibitors

The "rationale" for off-campus placement of all practica and internship students can be convincing (e.g., proper placement of students by major interest; availability of experienced, "real-time" clinicians to supervise and mentor neophytes; access to a variety of clients who are prescreened for appropriate placement with a counselor trainee; and access to a variety of other specialists from whom trainees can learn and consult). All of this can be accomplished while diminishing to some degree the concerns with liability, ethical, and financial issues. Such a practice is time-, personnel-, and dollar-efficient. Higher education administrators like this kind of thinking. Likewise, there is the added load reduction to the faculty that permits greater attention to grant writing, publications, and research.

Although undoubtedly there are more inhibitors to meeting the CACREP standards for a laboratory facility, those listed previously represent ones common to most programs, large and small. There are worthy reasons for overcoming these inhibitors, however. An on-campus laboratory can provide opportunities for better counselor preparation in the future.

Advantages of On-Campus Laboratory Training

Technically, a counselor education program may meet the CACREP standards for providing a facility by demonstrating that: (a) space is available for individual and group work; (b) resources are available for assessment, career, educational, and sociopersonal counseling; and (c) the faculty have some control of the use of the space as it relates to counselors in training. Access to mircocomputers may not necessarily mean exclusive dedication to counseling purposes (i.e., the computers may be found in an adjacent media or career center that serves other students and programs).

The reference here to the "spirit" of the standards is twofold. First, as chair (from 1981 to 1987) and a member of the CACREP council, the author attempted to interpret the standards as a guide to what might be considered basic practice. If an institution's faculty could demonstrate that it satisfied or exceeded the standards by outcome measures that were found acceptable to graduates, supervisors, employers, visiting team members, and the council, many of the specific statements in the standards needed to be considered as "advisory" rather than obligatory, per se. Standards should not be used as an inflexible yardstick, but as a guide to acceptable practice within a broad context of possible alternatives. Therefore, meeting or exceeding a specific standard could be demonstrated by more than one means. This was to meet the spirit of the standards.

The council is often asked, in how many standards can you have deficiencies and still get accredited? The author's answer to that question is, if you have to ask, you probably have too many! On the one hand, the council must render its judgment about any standard in a frame of reference that not only allows but encourages innovation, creativity in overcoming inhibitors, and resourcefulness in striving to do the best job possible with counselor preparation. On the other hand, it is the responsibility of the faculty seeking accreditation to demonstrate that it strives to exceed the standards and meet the spirit of the standards through excellence as a nationally accredited program.

The following list of advantages of maintaining a counseling laboratory where real counselees are served by both faculty and students, including advanced master's candidates and doctoral students, is provided with the intention of promoting excellence in preparation

1. Brings Mainstream Counseling Services into Preservice Preparation

Although most counselor educators today have practiced as professional counselors, unless they continue to "practice," they tend to lose the immediacy of a case load and the most current issues related to new methods, the sense of responsibility for the care of counselees, and the perspective of a caregiver. Even co-counseling provides many opportunities to stay in touch with these and other issues common to the practitioner. Equally important, students have the opportunity to discuss cases with the faculty and other students who can observe and participate in the process while they are still on campus. As a consequence, theory and practice can be blended together in both academic and experiential classes far more readily.

2. Encourages Research on Methods of Counseling and Supervision

The CACREP standards make reference to the need for both faculty and students to engage in and use research in their professional activities. However, meeting this expectation except by reading about the research of others can be a major hurtle for students and faculty alike. There can be a natural and readily available source of research interests when a counseling clinic is within walking distance of classrooms and faculty offices. One-way mirrors and videotape equipment are only part of the tools now facilitating direct access to research topics, including those associated with counseling supervision. Computer software for career assessment and planning; appraisal instruments and techniques for use with individuals, couples, and families; and intervention strategies for various populations all lend themselves to studies well defined and delimited to the practicalities of academic terms and limited financial resources. By modeling such activity during the academic training phase of neophytes' preparation as professionals, they can learn how to incorporate the attitudes, methods, and techniques of the scientist into their repertoire as a practitioner.

3. Creates Opportunities for Collaboration

By virtue of the fact that a community service is provided through the counseling clinic, schools, agencies, business and industry, and other university departments are logical partners for seeking external grants and contracts related to training, research, and consultation. There must be sensitivity to the political realities of existing funding sources and the willingness of other agencies to embrace a new competitor for such funds (e.g., from limited community sources). On the other hand, state, federal, and foundation grants can be enhanced by consortia composed of units that complement one another's assets. Students can be involved in grant writing, service delivery, and research activities on a variety of levels. These could be the very skills and knowledge that make them most versatile and competitive in the job market upon graduation. In addition, it places both faculty and students in a position to be knowledgeable about and helpful to those agencies with which students and graduates will be working in the future.

4. Students Can Practice Supervision as Well as Consultation Under Faculty Direction

When the services of a clinic include sufficient counselee loads to permit regular observation and supervision of actual counseling on a regular basis, the opportunity for greater attention to supervision and consultation is improved. Doctoral and advanced master's students can learn techniques and methods from observation and participation by direct faculty supervision and demonstration. As higher expectations are placed on counselors to supervise and consult with others using their specialized knowledge and skills, it becomes all the more important that they learn at least some of these essential skills in their master's degree programs and, for doctoral students, prior to completion of the terminal degree. In many programs today, such opportunities are incidental to the main curriculum, if they are available at all.

5. Permits Modeling of Collaboration and Open Discussion of Issues Related to Counseling Services

Diagnosis, treatment planning, intervention methods, ethical and legal issues, and matters related to the administration of a counseling service become immediate and relevant content based on what is going on in the clinic. Unlike a community or other external agency where policies and practices are to be learned but not discussed, a preservice, university-based clinic can function as a teaching facility with deliberate opportunities provided for open dialogue about all issues relevant to the conduct of effective counseling services. Naturally, there can be just as closed a system in a counselor education clinic if the faculty do not conceptualize its availability as an especially unique source of such issues for the students.

6. Enriches Other Aspects of the Curriculum

This advantage, much like the last, is a statement of philosophy and value. It is predicated on the observation of 30 years as a counselor educator that too many colleagues learn to talk and teach about counseling rather than participate in and model what they teach. In fact, some, if not many, are actually resistant to being observed behind the same mirrors, video cameras, and role-play situations in which students are expected to practice their new skills and knowledge. Having access to a clinic in which they can continue to hone and practice their skills will not only reduce the resistance but actually obviate it because it is easier to teach from current practice than from recollections in the far distant past. On the other hand, it must be a priority of the program and encouraged as a faculty activity for it to become a truly integral part of the total curriculum.

Summary

The essential underlying message within the previous text might be summarized as follows: The standards related to clinical facilities have received little attention in the past for a variety of reasons, some of which are listed previously. Access to furnished space, technical and clerical assistance, and counseling resource materials are significant but not insurmountable challenges to meeting the standards. Many programs have access to university resources that help them meet the "letter" of the standards' requirements sufficiently well to satisfy the CACREP council's expectations. In fact, one notable point in support of this observation is that, throughout the history of the standards and their revisions, no one has ever suggested eliminating this section of the standards. If this had been a major block to accreditation, this section would have been addressed much sooner.

The spirit of the standards, which, in the author's opinion, concerns excellence, might be interpreted to suggest that more practice by students and faculty could and should take place in such a clinic. "To demonstrate and model" (see standards' statements in appendices) counseling in a university clinic by those of us who teach about it in didactic courses can be a powerful, positive learning experience for all students at all levels of preparation. In short, the benefits could be substantial. However, there are a number of inhibitors that mitigate against such a wholehearted embracing of the possibilities of the standards. Some of these are attitudinal on the part of the faculty; some are structural within higher education because of limited resources and a reward system that tends not to equate such services with publications, teaching, research, and grant writing.

This may bring counselor educators to a philosophical and practical dilemma. Do we continue to get by with the minimum required by the standards, or are we committed to attaining the highest levels and best methods of teaching that we can reach? Some may say that, through their private practices, they can achieve at least some of the benefits noted earlier without the hassles of the other inhibitors. This may be true. However, private practices are not principally engaged in for teaching purposes, and therein lies a significant difference.

The positive benefits can outweigh the inhibitors if the faculty as a whole supports the commitment to a fully functioning clinic and makes use of its many lessons in the classroom and seminars. Elsewhere in this book are chapters that elaborate further the challenges and benefits of clinics. In the past, we have debated issues related to: (a) ratios of faculty to students in practica, (b) number of hours for practica and internship, and (c) the merits of greater or lesser specificity of types of experiences and competencies to be mastered. We also might ask, how can we encourage university administrators and counselor educators to embrace the spirit of the standards such that, in coming years, counselor education students will have the opportunity not only to be supervised doing at least some counseling on campus, but also have the opportunity to observe, critique, and co-counsel with a faculty member? The makers of our national standards have left us a legacy. Are we to hold to what was envisioned 30 years ago, or are we expected to respond to the changes in our students and society?

Implications

1. ACES has the opportunity to establish a committee to study counselor education clinics and their implications for the quality of counselor

preparation. Such a committee should be charged with collecting research data that could guide the development of future standards for recommendation to CACREP. To do otherwise begs the question of their value as proposed in this chapter.

2. The directors of clinical training and clinics have an opportunity to document and articulate the benefits and challenges associated with their activities. This book is an excellent beginning to this process.

3. Counselor educators, individually and collectively, can ask themselves, do I learn best by lecture, example, or both? The answer for most will be, both. The same is true for students. If not through a clinic, can we find more ways to model and demonstrate such that our students have the best opportunities for their learning?

4. Finally, if counselor educators are not the ones providing direct supervision to our students in their practica, what do we know of those who do? Is there more that we, individually and/or collectively through ACES, can do to ensure that students have the best knowledge, skills, and judgment modeled in their first professional-practice experiences?

References

Bobby, C. L., & Kandor, J. R. (1992). Assessment of selected CACREP standards by accredited and non-accredited programs. *Journal of Counseling and Development, 70,* 677–684.

Hollis, J. W., & Wantz, R. A. (1990). *Counselor preparation: Programs, personnel, trends.* Muncie, IN: Accelerated Development.

Vacc, N. A. (1992). An assessment of the perceived relevance of the CACREP Standards. *Journal of Counseling and Development, 70,* 685–687.

PART II

CLINIC DIRECTORS' ROLES AND RESPONSIBILITIES

CHAPTER 5

THE POSITION OF CLINIC DIRECTOR

Richard A. Wantz

Counselor education clinic directors assume a variety of roles in the course of their work. Their specific responsibilities are related to the needs and resources of the department and university, as well as the philosophy of training of the counselor education program. In this chapter, the varied roles, responsibilities, and issues encountered by a director of a counselor education laboratory or clinic are explored. Included are discussions of the importance of a mission statement to guide the development of the directorship, and a job description for the director. The job description evolved from the author's experiences directing clinics in three different universities over a span of 15 years.

Establishing a Mission Statement

An initial focus of a director is to establish and clarify a mission statement. The mission statement likely will include a description of the following: (a) purpose, (b) goals, (c) intervention philosophy, (d) scope of activity/practice, (e) professional identification, (f) licensure board requirements, (g) hours of operation, and (h) extent of liability. The definition of these topics is required by university administrators and sets the tone for the direction and future of a clinic. In the author's experience, the primary purpose of the clinics is to provide a teaching facility for counselor education programs. A clinic enables graduate students to

Note. Susan K. Spille, graduate clinical coordinator at the Wright State University Office for Counseling and Life Planning Services, made conceptual and editorial contributions to this chapter.

integrate and apply theory with practice. In addition, the clinic provides services to individuals from the surrounding community and affords research opportunities for the faculty and students.

The purpose, scope of practice, and clientele targeted can become significant issues with other campus clinics (e.g., psychology, education) and practitioners located in the surrounding community. Politically, most state universities do not want to send a message that the institution's services, which are subsidized by tax dollars, are intentionally competing with the private-business sector.

Professional identification may be a challenge for programs that prepare psychologists and counselors. Some university faculty have found it difficult to maintain a perspective of equality between the two professions. Most licensure boards define the scope of practice and the type of supervision required for supervised experience.

All students and supervisors working at a training clinic should be required to maintain professional liability insurance. In addition, the clinic director should confirm the extent that litigation will be covered by the university and/or state (for state-funded institutions). The possibility of litigation, as discussed in chapter 10, has a significant effect on the mission statement, and both affect the roles required of the director.

The Job Description of the Director

A clinic director must develop and orchestrate a description of duties, responsibilities, and roles essential for quality training and clinical services. The duties, which are eventually etched out by the counselor education faculty, may range from coordinator and maintainer to director and builder. An important consideration for becoming a clinic director is the institution's criteria for promotion and tenure. Clearly the institution's criteria must recognize and value clinic responsibility. One needs to determine if the clinic director is also the program's training director. I view the two responsibilities as closely related, but not synonymous. For example, the training director may be more concerned with sequencing counselor education and the development of skilled helpers, whereas the clinic director may focus on providing a rich forum where training can occur. Some of the major duties of the director, discussed next, are: (a) funding agent, (b) facility coordinator, (c) equipment manager and technician, (d) personnel administrator, (e) client-procurement agent, (f) documentation inspector, (g) researcher, and (h) public-relations specialist.

Funding Agent

A responsibility of a clinic director is to secure adequate funds and support to operate the clinic. Ideally, a counseling-training clinic would be fully supported financially by the parent institution. It will not surprise individuals working in academia that the institution's fiscal officers are not looking for locations to park unused funds. Expenses span the gamut of salary for a director, often operationalized as released time, graduate assistants, support staff such as receptionists and/or secretaries, resources, telephone, postage, computer programs (e.g., word processing, evaluation instruments—Microtest Assessments from suppliers such as National Computer Systems and Consulting Psychologists Press), and equipment (e.g., video and audio recording units, computer(s), printer(s), and scanners). Usually, the department housing the counseling clinic will underwrite all or some portion of these expenses. Viable sources of additional funding include: (a) client fees, (b) contracting to provide services to local children and adult services agencies and university alumni, and (c) external and institutional competitive grant programs.

Facility Coordinator

A wide range of options must be evaluated when considering the physical arrangements of the facility. Some of the issues a clinic director must appraise include: (a) a convenient and accessible location; (b) compliance with the Americans with Disabilities Act; (c) building and personal security; (d) parking convenience for clients and staff; (e) sound-proofed office space for counselors, supervisors, program faculty, the clinic director(s), and clinical activities (e.g., individual and group counseling, play therapy, relaxation, and biofeedback rooms); (f) a reception area; (g) assessment and evaluation space; (h) media and resource library; (i) electronics (e.g., wiring for video and/or audio recording, computer networking, phone to call into counselors during live supervision sessions and/or bug-in-the ear, observation windows); (j) storage for equipment such as play-back units on four-wheel carts; and (k) a secure location for client files. Space is required for counselors to wait for their clients' arrival and to complete case documentation. Ideally, space will be provided to facilitate counselor preparation for interventions and case documentation, and to encourage discussion, research, and study among staff while they wait for clients. The building entrance and exit and the client waiting room need to be designed and maintained so clients have a sense of confidentiality and comfort.

Equipment Manager and Technician

Some of the major equipment item considerations include: (a) audio and video recording and play back, (b) computer system(s) with modem, (c) printer(s), (d) direct connection to the institution's main frame(s), (e) an optical mark reading (OMR) document scanner, (f) computer applications (word processing, spread sheets and databases, assessment report generation, client file management, and accounting), and (g) biofeedback. Maintenance and repair agreements for equipment may become a significant expense. Some institutions (e.g., Indiana University) have successfully entered into partnerships with manufacturers of equipment to fulfill this need.

Personnel Administrator

Staffing needs may be broken out into four areas: (a) administration, (b) supervision, (c) clinical services, and (d) housekeeping. Administrators would include the director(s), receptionist(s), often a work-study student, and one or more graduate assistants. Selecting support staff who have the necessary skills often is a problem with work-study students. It is vital for all staff to demonstrate ownership and responsibility for the challenges of advancing the clinic. Recruitment procedures and selection criteria need to be developed for counselors, who will provide direct services to a variety of clientele. Supervisors must have appropriate professional credentials and might include advanced graduate student(s), program alumni, adjunct(s), and/or faculty. Dr. Joseph F. Maola and the faculty at Duquesne University have implemented an effective supervisory relationship between credentialed program alumni and counselor trainees in the program's clinic. It is critical that supervisors be in compliance with state-licensure guidelines. Housekeeping is usually provided by the institution. In addition, an orientation program will be required at the beginning of each academic term to ensure that counselors, supervisors, and support staff have an accurate understanding of established clinic policies and procedures. Staff at all levels may participate in the orentiation.

Client-Procurement Agent

The targeted client population can become an important issue to the institution's central administration, departments, and units on campus that feel territorial boundaries are being violated. For example, the institution's student-affairs staff (the career-planning unit and the counseling center) may feel uncomfortable with a separate counseling clinic offering similar services to students. Thus, clients may need to be recruited from off campus. Once the client population is clearly defined and approved, efforts to recruit clients, market the services offered, and maintain positive public relations need to be implemented. Providing quality services will make this task less time-consuming and laborious. An effective client-screening and intake procedure must be maintained, as well as criteria for conducting mental status examinations and making referrals. Other client issues include: (a) crisis-intervention procedures, (b) fee structure if not a free service, (c) maintenance of records, and (d) quality assurance.

Documentation Inspector

Documentation procedures and forms are critical issues. A good resource for forms is the *Practicum and Internship Textbook for Counseling and Psychotherapy* (Boylan, Malley, & Scott, 1988). At the clinic directed by the author, the following forms have been developed or secured: (a) Personal Data (for initial intake), (b) Intake and Initial Interview and an Intake Checklist, (c) Mental Status Examination (adopted from the Ohio Department of Mental Health), (d) Client's Rights and Grievance Procedures (ACA has a good model), (e) Client Fee Schedule, (f) Informed Consent and Information, (g) Process Notes, (h) Progress Notes, (i) Treatment Plan, (j) Diagnostic Summary, (k) Control Sheet (for client folders), (l) Involuntary Hospitalization, (m) Authorization for Release of Information, (n) Application for Practicum (for counseling students), (o) Counselor Education Supervision Agreement guidelines, and (p) recruitment letters (sample included in Appendix E). All forms developed at the author's institution are scrutinized by legal department personnel who have made very beneficial suggestions. To avoid potential liability, Process Notes are removed from client files and become the property of the student counselor at the time of termination.

Researcher

It is important to consider the extent to which the clinic will provide research opportunities for faculty and students. In the author's experience, clinical training, quality service, and research opportunities focusing on outcome effectiveness have complemented the overall quality of clinics. Institutional human-subject guidelines must be followed when conducting research with clients, counselors, or supervisors.

Public-Relations Specialist

Open communications and maintenance of supportive professional relationships with colleagues and referral sources such as community agencies, schools, and human-service professionals are essential. A director may be called to make presentations and speeches to community agencies, the media, schools, and organizations.

Summary

The major roles, responsibilities, and issues encountered by the author while involved with counselor education clinics were identified in this chapter. Each institution provides a different mix of challenges. A clinic director must serve multiple masters concurrently: (a) counselor trainees, (b) supervisors, (c) program faculty, (d) institutional administrators, (e) clients, (f) researchers, and (g) referral sources.

Addressing the issues outlined in this chapter increases the probability of success. At most institutions, this activity requires more time than one is released from instruction. Thus, effective management skills of time, tasks, materials, people, and crisis are essential for survival. Being a clinic director can be very rewarding clinically, personally, and professionally. Counselor trainees appreciate receiving quality supervision and relevant clinical experience. The rewards greatly outweigh any additional commitment of time and effort.

Implications

1. The CACREP standards and ACA ethical standards, when appropriate, should address the following issues:
   a. The roles of the director of counselor education training and the clinic or laboratory director should be delineated. Clinic work assignments should be understood by departmental colleagues and university decision makers.
   b. Promotion, tenure, and merit pay criteria should acknowledge the energy and time commitment required for managing a laboratory or clinic, and the basis for rewarding exemplary performance for these responsibilities should be specified. Guidelines for assigning teaching, scholarship, service, and clinic management assignment responsibilities should be provided.

   c. The credentials of the clinic or laboratory director should be specified. Clinic directors should be credentialed by the National Board for Certified Counselors (NCC) and state counseling licensure boards, if such a license exists. Specialty NCC credentials should be encouraged (e.g., Certified Clinical Mental Health Counselor [CCMHC], National Certified Career Counselor [NCCC], National Certified Gerontological Counselor [NCGC], and National Certified School Counselor [NCSC]).

   d. Funding and staffing should be adequately provided for clinic operations, supervision, staffing, and facilities.

2. Counselor education clinic policies, procedures, and documentation forms should be reviewed and approved by the university administration and legal personnel prior to implementation.

3. The clinic director is ultimately responsible for a variety of tasks and is accountable for various roles if the clinic is to be successful. Directing a clinic requires business management skills including: (a) motivator, (b) enforcer of policy, (c) problem solver, and (d) counselor. Selection of an effective clinic director should reflect these management skills.

4. My experience has been that students receive better supervision and a more organized and comprehensive experience at counselor education clinics than they receive from off-campus locations. Guidelines for off-campus practicum sites should be strengthened.

References

Boylan, J. C., Malley, P. B., & Scott, J. (1988). *Practicum and internship textbook for counseling and psychotherapy.* Muncie, IN: Accelerated Development.

CHAPTER 6

CLINIC DIRECTORSHIP: A MULTIFACETED ROLE

Rex Stockton

Most helping professionals do not learn how to operate a training clinic in their graduate training. In 1970, the author became actively involved in clinic instruction at the Indiana University Center for Human Growth, a departmentally staffed campus/community counseling center that serves as a training center for master's students in counselor education and doctoral students in counseling psychology.

Although there are some notable exceptions, when the author became clinic director there were few counterparts in other counselor education training programs. Operating an on-campus training clinic by academic departments has a fairly short history. The establishment of training centers in clinical psychology was endorsed by the 1966 Chicago Conference on Professional Preparation of Clinical Psychologists (Hoch, Ross, & Winder, 1966). However, it was not until at least the later 1980s that a widespread interest in on-site clinic services in counselor education departments emerged. Thus, in most cases, it has been a relatively short span of time since clinics became an integral part of training programs. Judging by the number of requests received by the author in the last 3 years from programs that wish to get started, it appears that they are beginning to flourish in training programs of the various helping professions.

Because there is such a paucity of literature on the topic of training centers, perhaps the way to start is with anecdotal reports. In this chap-

Note. Grateful acknowledgment is due to Lisa Hornibrook for assistance in preparing this manuscript.

ter, the author's personal experience is highlighted to illuminate some of the roles and responsibilities that seem most salient for clinic directors.

Roles of the Director

As with the administration of any organization, especially small ones, the director must carry out multiple roles. In this regard, working within a university setting presents many opportunities and challenges. In addition to instruction, university roles include research and service. In addition to his or her administrative role, the director often has to prove him or herself as an academic and a researcher. A 1982–1983 survey by Calhoun and Green (1984) of psychology clinic directors indicated that the modal director was a tenure-line faculty member who spent half of his or her time administering the clinic. Although this is obviously a major investment of time, research has more status than clinical training. Thus, the training director may find that other faculty are not enthusiastic about involvement in the training program. Minutes of a meeting of clinic directors at the Western Psychology Association/Rocky Mountain Psychology Association in 1989 reflect the consensus and concern of directors that, in most universities, clinical work is less likely to be rewarded than research (Cross & Spruill, 1989).

Clinic directors often must negotiate with faculty to provide supervision and must ensure standards of quality while honoring the academic freedom of the faculty member. This can require good negotiating skills. Clinic directors can be sure that they will be held legally responsible for the quality of their service, but many times do not have input in who will be providing service and supervising the trainees. Sometimes this can be a classic case of having responsibility without authority. Although there are many responsibilities with which clinic directors are concerned, a selection of topics to be discussed next are: (a) resource development, (b) the importance of staff, and (c) the quality of service to the consumer.

Resource Development

Although clinic directors have many and varied responsibilities, they must be concerned first of all with resources. Without resources, even the best planned and staffed programs cannot succeed. When the author acquired the directorship of a departmentally staffed campus/community counseling center, the center had been in operation for 7 years, therefore it already had a history. However, it was soon discovered that funds were needed to begin the semester. In other words, before there could be any strategic planning or organizing, there had to be enough resources to open the doors for the fall semester; this was done by securing a loan.

After this difficult experience, the need to make the clinic economically viable became a priority. To do this, several things had to take place. First of all, an advisory board consisting of the director and several faculty and public-spirited citizens organized to derive strategies to broaden the financial base. Over the years, this same group continued to meet to review organizational plans for the center and to represent the center's work to the community at large.

Because client fees were minimal, and for many years the university provided almost no direct line budget, other resource-development strategies had to be adopted. Over the years, fund-raising strategies included: (a) approaching foundations and trusts for funds, (b) holding fund-raising events including an annual benefit, and (c) sending an annual letter to center-trainee alumni requesting donations.

In the author's experience, if one offers a service to the community, one can expect that the community will respond with help when properly asked. Thus, graduates of the program who received a significant portion of their clinical training at the center are often quite willing to contribute on a yearly basis. This is especially true after they have become settled in their careers.

In the author's clinic, until recently, virtually all funds have had to come from sources other than the university. Fortunately, the university has seen fit to begin to subsidize a more significant portion of the clinic's operating cost. No matter where the funds come from, anyone who directs a clinic will discover early on that one primary role is to secure resources, not just manage them.

The Importance of Staff

In a people-serving agency, the most important resource is the staff. Thus, a primary concern to a clinic director has to be the quality of staff with whom he or she works. In a clinic, there are direct service, support, and administrative staff. From the beginning, emphasis must be placed on selecting staff who are willing to work in an environment that provides services to the public while serving as a training center.

Students

For the most part, the counseling staff in a training center are professionals in training (i.e., graduate students eager to have a real-life experience). In the author's clinic, there was (fortunately) a large pool of counselors eager for training positions from which to choose. Thus, it has generally been regarded as an honor to be selected as a practicum student at the Center for Human Growth. Although this helps to ensure quality staff and high morale, the selection process becomes another time-consuming job for someone; in this case, the clinic director.

Supervisors

Although it is important to tap into students' idealism and energy level, a quality experience for the students as well as their clients includes appropriate supervision. In our credentialed society, this means supervision needs to be done by licensed professionals. In our case, we were able to use both counseling faculty and area professionals who were willing to work on an adjunct basis.

The policy at the author's clinic was that all sessions be video or audio taped, and that counselors in training receive a significant amount of one-to-one and group supervision. The director does not have to do all of the supervision, but must make sure that an appropriate training sequence be available to all counselors to ensure quality service and quality training.

Area professionals have also served through the provision of weekly presentations. These included current topics that students would not be exposed to in depth in class, such as AIDS, eating disorders, and so on, or topics adding specialized training to that which students have been exposed, such as family systems, substance abuse, or more in-depth *DSM-III* knowledge. Here again, the director, either directly or through supervision of others, is responsible for the planning of topics and recruitment of qualified individuals. On occasion, this process has included a pickup and delivery service for speakers in bad weather, a baby-sitting service for a speaker who was unable to present without care for his or her child, and physically reserving a parking space by having someone stand there until the speaker arrived.

Administrative and Support Staff

The administrative staff in training clinics usually means secretarial staff and, if the director is lucky, an assistant. The author was blessed with excellent secretaries and advanced doctoral students who, after completing their initial clinical training, could serve as assistant directors. As in any organization, there are many logistical activities that staff members must perform. Clients must be greeted, appointments made, telephones staffed, records kept, and letters sent, all in an efficient and timely manner.

Most important, in addition to efficiency, support staff must have sensitivity. Although it is crucial to have well-developed plans and procedures for both normal activity and emergency situations, these procedures must be carried out by people. Often support staff get heavily involved in this activity; they very often are at the front line of contact with clients and the public. No matter how carefully clients are screened, emergency situations will occur. These may be anything from a suicidal client to one having a psychotic episode. Even if the agency refers on this type of client, when they present themselves they must be handled with care and compassion. Good support staff know when to call for help immediately, or when to make other judgments. The director cannot be available for every emergency and often must work through others. Thus, the recruitment and selection of quality support staff is of primary importance. A corollary with this is the setting up of an appropriate administrative structure that truly facilitates the mission of the agency.

Policies and Procedures

Critical to the quality of services offered by the training center are well-articulated policies and procedures. These include such areas as: (a) administrative and practicum staff responsibilities, (b) training and supervision policies, (c) kind of clients the clinic accepts, (d) referral policies, (e) emergency procedures, (f) fee structure, and (g) other important areas. The author found it important to enunciate policies at the Center for Human Growth into both a practicum manual and an administrative manual.

A well-developed training curriculum and supervisory experience is critical to the success of a program. The role of the director often goes beyond administration and includes involvement in instruction and supervision. In addition to regular supervision, this often means serving as a backup supervisor for emergencies that can occur at very late hours.

Service

A training center cannot exist solely for the benefit of the professionals in training. Without clients, there can be no training. Thus, training and service are inextricably intertwined.

It is incumbent on the director to see that clients are well cared for. This means having some system of quality control for counselor supervision, appeal procedures when the counseling is not working out, and contact with referral sources who often want to know what happened with their client. Additionally, procedures for referral must include liaisons with other agencies and helping professionals, such as psychiatrists, for backup and referral.

Training centers are frequently called on for consultation services both on and off campus. This provides training opportunities as well as service to the community. However, consultation can be time-consuming. Again the director has to play an active role in determining which requests can be met and in selecting, training, and supervising staff who carry out the consultation.

Another important aspect is maintaining relationships with key individuals as well as other agencies and the community. The director is often called on to represent the agency; much of the agency's credibility is based on how successful the director is in this activity. In the view of outsiders, the director is the center. Having friends and allies can be critical at any moment, especially in clinics.

Summary

In this chapter, the multiple roles of the director and the delicate situation in which directors sometimes find themselves have been discussed. The importance of (a) developing resources, (b) working with staff, (c) articulating appropriate policies and procedures, (d) placing a priority on service to clients, and (e) managing the intricacies of working in an academic environment have all been considered. Any recounting of the roles of the director runs the danger of making it appear that responsibilities far outweigh the rewards. However, this is simply not the case.

The first and probably most long-lasting reward is the intensive contact with students in their formative clinical development. This is often followed up with pleasurable exchanges with former students many years later. Also, having a client population available for research studies can be extremely helpful in developing a long-term research program for individual faculty. Finally, the author found that the challenge of helping an organization to perform effectively, despite inevitable difficulties, was gratifying.

Major Implications

For counselor education programs, training clinics are a relatively new phenomenon. Several considerations to examine are:

1. They are an important resource for providing a clinical experience for graduate student trainees that can be overseen by faculty.
2. It is possible for them to support research efforts, particularly involving counseling efficacy and training issues.
3. They can also provide an important direct service to the community.

However, training clinics come with costs. These include:

1. The effort required to organize and maintain them.
2. Because their function is more than academic, they do not fit easily into a departmental structure.
3. Faculty often do not feel that they are rewarded for their service commitment to clinic training.

In terms of the clinic director's roles, there are several considerations to examine. These include:

1. The training-clinic director must be prepared to function in multiple roles simultaneously.
2. Clinic directors must be concerned about resource development as well as resource management.
3. The ability to select and work effectively with staff at all levels is critical.
4. Clinic policies and procedures need to be clearly articulated.
5. The clinic director must pay attention to the quality of the service as well as the quality of training.

Although this book is a good first step, we do not yet have enough reports from successful (and unsuccessful) clinic experiences. Additional time and attention should be given to developing more literature and encouraging special-interest groups and conferences regarding this topic. The fundamental question of the best mechanism to provide clinical experiences for students in counseling needs continual attention.

References

Calhoun, J. F., & Green, C. (1984). Perspectives of psychology training clinics from training and clinic directors. *Professional Psychology: Research and Practice, 15*(3), 371–378.

Cross, H., & Spruill, J. (1989). *Association of directors of psychology training clinics, Newsletter #21.* Pullman, WA: Washington State University Press; University, MS: University of Southern Mississippi Press; University, AL: University of Alabama Press.

Hoch, E.L., Ross, A.O., & Winder, C.L. (Eds.). (1966). *Professional preparation of clinical psychologists.* Washington, DC: American Psychological Association.

CHAPTER 7

REACTION: PLANNING FOR CLINICAL DIRECTORSHIP

Susan B. DeVaney

As a counselor educator working in a nondoctoral-granting university without the advantage of a counselor-training clinic, I read Stockton and Wantz with competing emotions. I have the utmost respect for the pioneers in the field who have built viable training centers, but at the same time I am dismayed at the difficulty of following their lead in the 1990s. This is an era of budget cutbacks, a time when employees in businesses throughout the country are being asked to put in overtime while their compatriots are laid off, and a time of state budget cuts for universities, frozen academic positions, and shrinking printing budgets.

At the same time, businesses (including those in the business of education) are being held increasingly accountable for their product and their process. Council for Accreditation of Counseling and Related Educational Programs (CACREP), the National Council for Accreditation of Teacher Education (NCATE), the Southern Association of Colleges and Schools (SACS), and other accrediting bodies; the state and federal governments; and universities are making more rigorous demands on individual faculty, departments, and colleges. The case-by-case, humanitarian approach, once widely used to manage problems, has increasingly become formal, written policy designed to meet various guidelines and accreditation standards. Cost-effectiveness of courses, programs, workshops, and conferences has become an increasingly more important element in program planning. Given the growing crunch of person power and resources, a university, college, or department must critically evaluate needs, resources, mission, and policy before organizing a clinical-training center. Two years

of preparation for CACREP accreditation, discussion with clinical directors, and brainstorming with faculty have led me to offer the following
observations concerning building a training center from scratch.

Funding and Organization

Initially, the desire to create a clinical-training center may arise from the
department head, the dean, or the faculty. Early discussions in project
planning generally begin with mission and move quickly to questions of
funding and organization. Would the center be designed to perform testing
and assessment? Developmental, career, or substance-abuse counseling?
Exactly what counseling service would be offered and to whom? How
would a stable client pool be developed? Would the clinic be designed
primarily as a vehicle for training, observing, and supervising selected
students? Would it serve as a center for supervised practice for all students, or for the administration of the clinical portion of the comprehensive exam? How many students would have an opportunity to work
in the center? How will they be chosen? Would faculty be expected (allowed, required) to counsel? Would their sessions be open to observation as training tools? Might faculty expect payment for counseling services
rendered? Where would clinic funding originate? How would research
factor into the equation?

Steering Committee

Brainstorming and conceptualization is what many academics do best.
However, once sufficient interest has been expressed, a project coordinator and steering committee are needed. Like any other small business, a
clinic must be planned and organized intelligently with an eye toward
economic and human-resource factors. The initial planning phase may
take a year or more, and will involve a sustained commitment of time
and effort. A successful project director will: (a) be tenured, (b) have
excellent relations with department colleagues, (c) have a history of service to the community, (d) demonstrate a collaborative administrative
style, and (e) possess commitment to clinical training. The job of project
coordinator should be understood to be a discrete function, with no plans
for the coordinator to become clinical director. Misunderstandings, charges
of empire building, and faculty apathy can largely be avoided when the
coordinator's function is to develop a plan that is workable independent

of a single individual. For this reason, the steering committee is best composed of members of the business, public school, university, and mental health communities.

The Clinic Self-Study

The year's self-study would culminate with a written proposal containing: (a) a needs analysis, (b) a survey of human and financial resources, (c) a mission statement, and (d) an administrative plan. The needs analysis is designed to address factors in the community, institution, and department justifying the operation of a training center. In the university community, many individuals and organizations may offer counseling services. A survey of target markets, schools, businesses, or general public should include a description of the particular assessment, testing, or counseling services the clinic might provide without duplication. Contracts between the center and a particular organization might eventually formalize an agreement for low-cost services in exchange for a steady flow of clients. Another crucial element of the proposal is a statement of current deficiencies in the counselor training program and proposed benefits (including dollars) accruing to the university, the program, and students with the advent of the clinical center. For example, if several programs (nursing, social work, psychology, counseling) are requesting funding for clinical experience, they might share facilities, thus satisfying many needs simultaneously.

Resource Assessment

No institution today can be expected to approve a major undertaking such as a clinical-training center, and no individual should agree to direct one, without a clear understanding of costs and available resources. One task of the project coordinator, and later the center director, is to determine what is necessary to run a center serving the identified target population. A second function is to pull together existing services to augment the training and counseling features of the clinic. A major task to be begun by the project coordinator and continued by the director is the building of relationships between the center and the community, the faculty, students, and the university administration with thought toward the concerns of these groups and ways they can support one another. These same agencies, individuals, or university departments may agree to: (a) provide equipment; (b) share personnel; (c) donate space, workshops, or other training; or (d) provide medical services. In the era of scarce resources, the center should be able to provide services and likewise take advantage of existing ones. Programs without a pool of cheap doctoral-student labor may develop a network of in-kind contributions or a system of referral exchange with local practitioners. Local counselors can be hired as student supervisors (adjunct faculty), part of whose job is to carry a client load and to be observed in action by students.

Commitment and Marketing

A fundamental component of the resource assessment, then, is letters of commitment from faculty, campus police, student counseling services, community practitioners, schools, churches, community agencies, individuals, and campus administrators. The process of obtaining commitments ensures that concerned parties (students, consumers, businesses, the mental health community, and authorities) are aware of the center and support its implementation. By the same token, clients cannot be expected simply to appear at the door, nor can they be expected to learn of the center and come to counseling because they have seen a brochure. It will be necessary to develop a marketing plan that includes agreements with agencies, schools, businesses, or churches for client referral. Through the process of formal discussion with concerned parties, the planning coordinator can (a) target the appropriate client population (i.e., one for which there is a large client pool and one that is suitable for the students in the counseling program), (b) ensure that instructional resources are not diverted to the center, (c) give faculty the option of committing supervision hours to the center, and (d) tap nontraditional resources for program management.

Policies and Procedures

The final section of the proposal involves policy and administration, matters fully addressed in principle by Wantz and Stockton. Sticky issues are best addressed concretely in the proposal. What provisions might be made for psychiatric emergencies? Is the clinical director legally responsible for all clients at all times? If so, to what extent does the university support the director in case of suit? To whom does the director answer? How binding are the suggestions of the steering committee? How does the responsibility of directorship affect promotion, tenure, and salary?

Job Descriptions

In addition, job description and division of labor must be outlined. Who is responsible for (a) soliciting contracts or partnerships from area businesses, (b) maintaining equipment, and (c) training clerical staff? Who writes the grants? What are the respective roles of (a) the steering committee, (b) the clinical director, (c) faculty, and (d) adjunct supervisors? What are the possibilities of obtaining funding for an administrative director who works alongside a clinical director, the clinical director being responsible only for training and supervision?

Budget

The final segment of the policy and procedures statement should also include a 5-year budget plan. Even the best-run businesses rarely make a profit in the first several years. Therefore, creative provision for the costs of operation through trade, sharing, or in-kind contribution may be called for in the center's early years, with increasing self-sufficiency later on.

Getting Started

Once the proposal is approved by the faculty and administration, a transitional period begins with the hiring or appointment of a clinical director. Because the project coordinator has remained in touch with those who have written letters of intent and informed them of the progress of the center, these persons are likely to deliver as promised. During this period of transition, the director and project coordinator work together. Collaboration and coordination are essential. Although center operation, with its incumbent administrative detail, is important, the director must maintain and nurture professional relationships with colleagues, community agencies, schools, and human service professionals. Indeed, the job described is a full-time endeavor, not one to be taken lightly or to be accepted along with an ambitious research agenda or a full teaching load.

Conclusion

However, one can conclude that with full consideration given to the experience of counselor educators in established clinical centers, it is possible to initiate new centers, even in bleak financial times and in nondoctoral-granting institutions. The keys to the magic gateway are: (a) preliminary planning, (b) creative management of resources, and (c) community collaboration—the components of successful program planning in the 1990s.

Chapter 8

REACTION: DEVELOPING A COUNSELOR EDUCATION LABORATORY AT BALL STATE UNIVERSITY

Roger L. Hutchinson

The effort to bring together those who have experienced the development of a counselor education laboratory, such as the author and those who want to do so, seems long overdue. Perhaps the following observations and suggestions, based on experiences at the Ball State University (BSU) Counseling Practicum Clinic, which was developed nearly a quarter of a century ago, will be helpful to others who might be contemplating the establishment of a counselor education laboratory.

The new Teachers College Building at BSU, which houses the Department of Counseling Psychology and Guidance Services, was built in 1967. The counseling facilities on the sixth floor include two large-group rooms, eight counseling cubicles, a waiting room, and audio and video capabilities. Prior to 1969, however, counselors in training went to other agencies to see their clients. Although a university counseling center already existed on campus, it was available only to students, faculty, staff, and their immediate families. At that time, the university counseling center was staffed by faculty with doctoral degrees; practicum students or interns were not allowed to see clients there. As a result, the logical thought process was: Why not develop a laboratory/clinic in the department and effectively utilize our new facilities? Why not invite folks from the surrounding area to come here for counseling, and at the same time provide practicum students with clients where they can be more effectively supervised by the regular counseling staff?

Needs-assessment letters were sent to agencies and schools within a 60-mile radius asking if they would be interested in BSU developing a clinic to complement their services. The response to the survey was overwhelming. Perhaps it was easier then because there were only a few counseling services available in the area. Consequently, established providers of counseling services felt less need to protect their turf.

The first director was given no released time to develop and direct the clinic. However, a doctoral student was assigned 20 hours a week to assist him. The director and student (a) made contacts with the public, (b) developed forms and procedures, (c) did all intakes, (d) made referrals, (e) responded to emergencies, and so on. It was impossible to anticipate the complications and pitfalls that would be encountered. On the other hand, tremendous satisfaction was realized from offering counseling services to 600–1,000 clients a year and providing an excellent learning opportunity to 60–70 master's students and 20–30 doctoral students each year.

When the BSU clinic was initially developed, the first shock was that psychiatrists in the area, who were tired of any-time-of-the-night calls from suicidal clients, dumped those clients on us. However, the faculty quickly came to the rescue, and developed a policy stating that all clients would be screened on intake, and that we would not accept clients beyond the expertise of students who were to be the counselors. Referral procedures were developed and arrangements made to refer such clients to other agencies.

Released time assigned to the director over the years has ranged from 0 time to two-thirds time, based on such factors as (a) the various department chairs' priorities, (b) change from quarter to semester system, and (c) resources available. Over the years, the director sometimes received two-thirds assigned time; the current director receives one-fourth clinic assigned time.

All forms (i.e., intake, transition to other counselors, termination, release of information) and procedures (i.e., regarding a possible subpoena, clients' rights to review their files, liability if clients are seen outside of clinic cubicles or transported) have been approved by university lawyers. All counselors are encouraged to carry their own liability insurance in addition to the university plan. Threats of lawsuits have been made, but none has been pursued to date. However, relevant questions might be: (a) Are the clinic director and practicum instructors responsible for student negligence? (b) Would lawyers be provided if we are sued? (c) If we lost a lawsuit, would any required cash settlement be covered by insurance?

The director must keep a reasonable balance between training and service. It is easy to lean toward service to clients. The director has sometimes needed a reminder that our reason for existing is to provide a training laboratory for students, and that we could not exist solely to provide counseling services to the community.

The director may feel that he or she has a lot of responsibility and very little authority. One quickly learns about "faculty autonomy," and may sometimes be surprised that (at least a few) experienced faculty who have lots of "good" suggestions are less than enthusiastic about becoming involved in the daily and frequently overwhelming responsibility of developing and maintaining the clinic. In other words, the director may often be faced with changes mandated by the department faculty but experience a lack of support in figuring out how to implement them in a rather complex structure.

Ongoing contacts with community agencies are essential so that referrals to and from these agencies can be coordinated. Networking between agencies (i.e., probation, welfare, child-protection services, schools, shelters, Comprehensive Mental Health, Crisis Hotline, children's homes) is important. Attempts to initiate regular meetings between these agencies is often difficult and complex. Unfortunately, agencies that regularly service the same client are often unaware that services are being duplicated.

The director must also negotiate arrangements with community agencies for clients' between-semester emergency needs (i.e., with Comprehensive Mental Health, Crisis Intervention). A related matter concerns what kind of contact to maintain between other than emergency-need clients and the clinic at this time. What contact, if any, should be made with clients who requested or had an intake interview before semester break and must wait 2–4 weeks for counseling? Should intakes even be done with these clients? If not, how does one meet the demand for additional clients for 30–50 students when the new semester begins?

Currently, practicum instructors are responsible for emergencies and consultation with student counselors on the day the practicum instructor's class meets, and these instructors also sign off on all reports. This relieves the director of considerable responsibility.

For many years, the clinic relied on volunteer receptionists or persons compensated by title programs (i.e., work/study programs, Council on the Aged). Gradually, additional doctoral students were assigned assistantship time to the clinic, and a half-time receptionist was funded by the university. Fortunately, the BSU Counseling Practicum Clinic, which is open from 8:00 a.m. to 9:00 p.m. Monday through Thursday and from 8:00 a.m. to 5:00 p.m. on Fridays, now has a full-time receptionist compensated by the university. More recently, several master's students volunteered time to the clinic. This furnishes us with needed help and provides students with good experiences in dealing with clients and the public.

The often-queried concern regarding the directorship of a counselor laboratory hindering promotion and tenure has not been true at BSU. The clinic has had two directors during the past 24 years; both have received early promotions and been tenured on track.

The clinic continues to provide an excellent training facility for students and offers a minimal-cost service to the community. Many graduates of our program have adopted procedures and have utilized BSU Counseling Practicum Clinic forms to develop counselor education laboratories throughout the United States and Europe. All in all, it has been and is a great experience. However, the following quote (Hutchinson, 1992) also expresses some of the possible frustration a director might experience:

> I've caught myself laughing aloud a few times lately and trying to figure out whether I'm going nuts or just taking things less seriously. For instance, after 19 years as founder and director of an outpatient clinic in our department where thousands of clients and hundreds of students have connected, I decided to retire from that responsibility—primarily because of my frustration with changes which didn't make sense to me. I unwisely anticipated gestures of appreciation from my peers for my many years of dedication to the clinic. I did feel appreciated by students, and they presented me with a card and a helium balloon during our last staffing of the year— my last as clinic director. As I walked to my car in the parking lot with a lump in my throat, the card under my arm, and the balloon tied to the handle of my brief case, I laughed aloud as I thought of how things had changed in 19 years and the hours of sweat and tears I had invested in this venture. My external reward was a card and a helium balloon. (pp. 456–457)

Reference

Hutchinson, R. L. (1992). The rules have changed, and I don't remember voting on it. *Journal of Counseling & Development, 70*(3), 456–457.

Part III

LEGAL AND ETHICAL ISSUES IN ON-CAMPUS CLINICS

Chapter 9

LEGAL ISSUES IN ON-CAMPUS CLINICAL TRAINING

Theodore P. Remley, Jr.

University faculty who administer on-campus clinics as a component of their graduate programs in counseling need to be aware of the many legal issues related to such training facilities. In universities where clinics already exist, faculty members should request through their administrators that the university attorney review their operations, policies, and procedures to ensure that they comply with university regulations and state and federal laws. If clinics are just being developed, faculty should consult with the university attorney as plans are being made.

Faculty should be concerned about malpractice issues and liability for all clinic participants. Informed consent of clients is very important in training facilities. Services to minors can be an issue when counseling for children or families is offered. If third-party reimbursement for services is utilized, there are many legal issues to be considered. Client confidentiality and records are very important legal aspects of clinic operations.

Malpractice

The legal concern expressed most often by faculty who administer on-campus clinics is their liability for malpractice that might occur in the training facilities. Although faculty should be aware of their liability, fear of being held accountable for harm done to clinic clients should not keep faculty from participating in and supporting on-campus clinics.

Under the common law of torts, individuals who interact with professionals have a legal right to be provided services in a manner that does not result in harm to them. If individuals are harmed by a professional, they may seek redress in a court of law by filing a malpractice lawsuit.

To prevail in a malpractice lawsuit, plaintiffs must demonstrate the following: (a) the professional had a professional relationship with them and therefore had a duty to care for them in a professional manner, (b) that duty of care was breached, (c) they were harmed as a result of the breach and can prove damages, and (d) the professional was the proximate cause of their damages (Woody, 1988).

Every organization or individual associated with an on-campus counseling clinic is responsible for the well-being of clients who are served by the facility. As a result, many entities and individuals could be sued for malpractice, including the university, the graduate department, clinic administrators, faculty members, clinical supervisors, and graduate students.

Most universities purchase professional liability insurance that covers the university in the event a malpractice lawsuit is filed. The insurance provides attorneys to handle the case and pays any settlement or judgment amount against the university. Occasionally, the insurance policies purchased by universities cover certain individuals as well. However, individual coverage in such policies is rare, and usually is limited to top-level administrators such as university presidents or vice presidents.

Because university professional liability policies cover only the institution, individuals associated with on-campus clinics need their own personal professional liability insurance policies. For their personal legal protection, clinic administrators, graduate program faculty, clinic supervisors, and graduate students should be encouraged to purchase professional liability insurance policies for themselves. There is no sound rationale for requiring clinic participants to have personal professional liability insurance policies. Administrators, faculty, and graduate students should be informed of their own personal liability and encouraged to purchase professional liability insurance policies, but they should not be required to do so.

Many professionals do not understand that if the university and a professional are both named as defendants in a professional malpractice case, that the legal interests of the institution and the professional may conflict. As a result, the attorney representing the university could act in such a manner that the professional who is employed or associated with the university could be put in a legally vulnerable position. As a result, when professionals are individually named in a malpractice lawsuit, it is vital that they have their own personal attorneys representing them and that they not rely on a university attorney to represent both them and the institution. Individual professional liability insurance policies ensure that professionals have personal attorneys representing them when they are named in lawsuits.

Graduate students who counsel clients within a counseling clinic are liable for any harm that they cause. However, others associated with the clinic are not only responsible for harm they cause, but they also are legally responsible for harm caused by those whom they supervise. Thus, faculty or advanced graduate students who serve as clinical supervisors are responsible for harm caused by the graduate student counselors they supervise. In addition, clinic administrators could be held accountable for any harm suffered by clients who come to the clinic. As a result, graduate programs that offer counseling-clinic services have a special interest in removing students who are not qualified for counselor training from their programs (Bradley & Post, 1991; Olkin & Gaughen, 1991).

Some states have total or partial sovereign immunity. Under sovereign immunity concepts, the state cannot be sued. If the immunity is partial, the state can be sued only up to a maximum amount. In states where sovereign immunity exists, individuals within state facilities still can be individually sued. As a result, it is vital for counseling-clinic administrators, faculty, and graduate students in institutions within states that have sovereign immunity to purchase individual personal professional liability insurance policies. For example, if a malpractice lawsuit was filed in a state in which sovereign immunity exists as a result of negligence that occurred in a university counseling clinic, the university and individuals within the clinic probably would be named as defendants. The university could file a petition to be dismissed as defendants because of sovereign immunity, and the court would grant the petition. This would leave only those who were individually named in the lawsuit to defend the suit on their own.

Informed Consent

Informed consent legal issues are becoming a major part of all professional counseling relationships, but are particularly important within university counseling-clinic settings. Basically, informed consent in a counseling context means that clients have consented to the counseling process after being fully informed of the nature, details, risks, and limitations of the relationship.

University counseling clinics must fully inform clients of the student status of counselors who are in training within the graduate program operating the clinic. It is inappropriate for clinics to mislead clients into thinking they are being provided services by fully qualified professional counselors if the counselor is a graduate student. Clinics do not have to draw excessive attention to the student status of counselors, but do have to fully inform clients in some fashion.

Minors are not legally able to give informed consent. As a result, informed consent forms need to be signed by parents or guardians for clients under the age of 18. For clients who are old enough to read and write effectively, it would be a good idea to ask them to sign informed consent forms in addition to the forms signed by their parents or guardians.

Services to Minors

There are no general common law principles that would lead to the conclusion that parental consent must be obtained by clinics before providing counseling services to minors. However, specific state statutes, federal regulations related to university funding, university regulations, or other guidelines that must be adhered to by clinics should be reviewed by an attorney to determine whether parental consent is required before offering counseling services to minors.

Although there could be state statutes or federal regulations to the contrary, it is likely that parents or guardians of minors would have a legal right to know the details of counseling sessions if they insisted (Salo & Shumate, 1993). However, to assert this right, parents or guardians would have to obtain a court order if the counselor refused to voluntarily disclose confidential information, and few people are willing to go to that extreme. On the other hand, the legal rights of parents and guardians must be understood when providing counseling services for minors. Parents and guardians probably also have a legal right to terminate counseling relationships with the minors under their control.

Minors do not have the legal capacity to contract (Bullis, 1993). As a result, clinics that charge fees could not legally collect fees from parents or guardians for services to minors, unless the parents or guardians had contracted on behalf of their children for the counseling services.

Third-Party Reimbursement for Services

Clinics that agree to complete health insurance forms to assist clients in obtaining reimbursement for counseling services must be careful to conduct themselves in a legal manner.

Clients must be told that a diagnosis indicating they have a mental or emotional disorder is required in order for them to apply for health insurance reimbursement, and that such a diagnosis will only be rendered if the professional counselor believes it is justified.

Clinics must be careful to avoid guaranteeing that a client's health insurance will reimburse them for clinic services. Clinics can agree to complete their parts of insurance claim forms, but cannot assure clients that an insurance company will reimburse.

When unsophisticated professionals engage in the health insurance reimbursement process without understanding it thoroughly, insurance fraud problems could occur. Clinic staff should ensure that clinic counselors, supervisors, and faculty are trained adequately, and that the process is monitored effectively. An insurance fraud problem could include criminal as well as civil penalties; it could ruin the reputation of a clinic, and cause the university extreme embarrassment.

Clinics must be careful to avoid the following practices that could be insurance fraud:

1. Telling the insurance company that direct health care is being provided by someone whose fees for services normally would be reimbursed when, in fact, the health care is being provided by someone whose fees for services normally would not be reimbursed.
2. Diagnosing a client solely to satisfy insurance company requirements when the diagnosis cannot be justified according to current professional knowledge and accepted practices concerning the diagnosis of mental illness.
3. Indicating on a bill that fees for services are a specified amount, but charging clients only the lesser amount reimbursed by the insurance company. For example, indicating that the fee for a session is $7, but accepting the 80% payment of $60 from the insurance company as payment in full.
4. Informing the insurance company that counseling services are being provided for an individual because only individual psychotherapy is reimbursable when services are actually being provided in a family, couple, or group situation.

5. Billing clients for hourly appointments that are missed, but not indicating on the bill that appointments were missed.
6. Failing to report previous contact with a client who has recently applied for health insurance reimbursement (Remley, 1993).

Confidentiality

Professional counselors have an ethical requirement to keep confidential information related to them by clients in counseling sessions (Arthur & Swanson, 1993). If the privacy rights of clients are violated through the unauthorized disclosure of confidential information, clients could sue for damages. In a university clinic, student counselors, supervisors, faculty members, clinic administrators, academic department administrators, other university administrators, and the university could be held accountable by clients whose privacy has been compromised.

In addition, there are situations in which clinics could be held accountable for failing to disclose information considered confidential. For example, if counselors make a professional determination that a client is a danger to self or others, counselors must take the least intrusive, but nevertheless effective, action to prevent the harm. In all jurisdictions, counselors are required by statute to report suspected cases of child abuse. Exceptions to confidentiality requirements are just as important as the general privacy rules.

Records

Clinic records must be kept in compliance with generally accepted practices of maintaining confidential records (Piazza & Baruth, 1990). Security is very important. Written authorizations should be required for releasing records, and clinic administrators should develop and monitor safe and effective record-keeping practices.

There are no common law rules related to the length of time counseling records must be kept. Administrative records that record appointments, payments, or general data must be kept separately from counseling case-note records. Generally, administrative records should be kept longer than case-note records. Records that document actions taken that may later protect counselors if accused of wrongdoing and records that could possibly be subpoenaed in the future should be kept as long as necessary. Other records should be destroyed in a systematic fashion. For example, all counseling case-note records for clients who have not been served within the last 2 calendar years might be destroyed each January 1st.

Counseling case-note records kept in the sole possession of the maker or made by a mental health professional for his or her own use in treatment are exempt from the Buckley Amendment requirement that students be allowed to review their educational records. However, all clinic records are subject to subpoena in certain circumstances, even when protected by a state-privileged communication statute. If a subpoena for records is received, legal counsel should always be consulted and his or her advice followed.

Conclusion

Only a few of the many legal issues that are of concern to university counseling-clinic administrators are summarized here. The advice of the university attorney should be sought in all situations involving legal matters.

Although legal issues should not inhibit university graduate programs from establishing or operating counseling clinics, legal responsibilities should be taken very seriously and clinic participants should be required to follow all established clinic procedures.

References

Arthur, G. L., Jr., & Swanson, C. D. (1993). *Confidentiality and privileged communication.* Alexandria, VA: American Counseling Association.

Bradley, J., & Post, P. (1991). Impaired students: Do we eliminate them from counselor education programs? *Counselor Education and Supervision, 31,* 100–108.

Bullis, R. K. (1993). *Law and management of a counseling agency or private practice.* Alexandria, VA: American Counseling Association.

Olkin, R., & Gaughen, S. (1991). Evaluation and dismissal of students in master's level clinical programs: Legal parameters and survey results. *Counselor Education and Supervision, 30,* 276–288.

Piazza, N. J., & Baruth, N. E. (1990). *Journal of Counseling and Development, 68,* 313–316.

Remley, T. P., Jr. (1993). You and the law. *American Counselor, 2*(2), 33, 35.

Salo, M. M., & Shumate, S. G. (1993). *Counseling minor clients.* Alexandria, VA: American Counseling Association.

Woody, R. H. (1988). *Fifty ways to avoid malpractice.* Sarasota, FL: Professional Resource Exchange.

CHAPTER 10

ETHICAL DILEMMAS AND COUNSELOR EDUCATION CLINICS: MORE QUESTIONS THAN ANSWERS

Robert H. Pate, Jr.

The subtitle statement that there are more questions than answers to questions about clinics operated as part of counselor education programs might strike the reader as yet another title phrase with more hyperbole than substance. A continued review of the literature and analysis of ethical codes and standards convinced the author that there is less substantive material on the operation of clinics as part of a counselor education program than any other critical element of counselor education. This conclusion was first reached when reviewing literature to prepare the presentation that resulted in this chapter. It initially appeared that the computer-search process had not been implemented properly, or that the right combination of terms from the thesaurus was not being used. Incredibly, multiple searches produced no relevant literature.

After numerous futile searches, the author was persuaded that the topic of the operation of clinics by counselor education programs was not adequately addressed in the literature of counseling. The available literature was concerned with clinics operated by psychology programs, and even that literature was scarce. It was tempting to mimic graduate students who delight in reporting a dearth of literature, but it still seemed that there must be literature on such an important topic. However, the author was finally satisfied that the problem was not the attempted searches when Myers and Smith (see chapter 1) reported of a similar lack of success. They stated:

> A literature search was conducted to ascertain the "state of the art" relative to counselor-training laboratories. It quickly became obvious that the overwhelming majority of available literature referred to psychology-training clinics, and that a paucity of literature exists relative to the operation of similar facilities within counselor preparation programs. (pp. 4–5)

With no significant body of literature to review, the focus was shifted to related topics, especially supervision and ethics, and to an informal inquiry directed to counselor educators who had experience with program-related clinics.

Although the literature of counseling supervision is growing, and most issues related to supervision per se are adequately addressed in that literature, a review of literature on supervision in counselor education also failed to provide any answers to questions that might be unique to the clinic operated by a graduate training program. The Association for Counselor Education and Supervision (ACES) *Handbook of Counseling Supervision* (Borders & Leddick, 1987) provided a comprehensive review and synthesis of counseling supervision, with more than 200 references. A review of the handbook, the titles of the references cited in the handbook, and the ACES Supervision Interest Network (1990) "Standards for Counseling Supervisors" did not provide answers to the questions faced by counselor education faculty members responsible for the operation of a counseling clinic. The "Ethical Standards" (American Counseling Association, 1988) govern counselors to not mention clinics or supervision in "Section H: Preparations Standards." Counseling ethical standards are not unique in their limited attention to supervision; the highly touted revision of the American Psychological Association Ethical Standards ("Ethical Principles," 1992) devoted only 6 lines to supervision and 60 lines to laboratory animals.

The importance of counseling clinics in a counselor education program was established by the Council for the Accreditation of Counseling and Related Educational Programs (CACREP) standard (III, D), which requires a counseling laboratory (a clinic) for an accredited program. However, the preceding standard (III, C) addresses off-campus practicum supervisors. Hence, although a demonstration facility is required by the CACREP standards, it is not a necessary component of the clinical instruction of counselor education students. The standards for both the practicum and internship include the phrase "regularly employed staff member," which suggests that a clinic operated by the program that had no regularly employed staff members would not be an appropriate practicum or internship setting. The cited CACREP standards are from the entry-level program standards; the doctoral program standards do not address the possibility of either a doctoral practicum or internship that occurs in a program-operated clinic. The purpose of this discussion of the CACREP standards is not to critique those standards, but to demonstrate that the ambiguity surrounding the proper role of clinics in a counselor education program is not limited to ethical issues—the major focus of this chapter.

The utility of the literature related to clinics operated by clinical psychology-training programs is limited because psychology clinics are typically organized as full-service mental health clinics and the students who are trained in such clinics are doctoral students. Much of the literature produced by searches for information about clinics addressed the topics of supervision and administrative issues in psychology-clinic management (e.g., dealing with third-party payers), not the ethical dilemmas that result from the confrontation of student training needs and client welfare.

Many of the issues that confront the counselor education program that operates or considers establishing a clinic to support its training program are administrative and legal. However, those issues are reviewed by other contributors and they are considered here only to the extent that they cannot be separated from the ethical focus of this chapter.

The Dilemmas

Clients

Securing Clients

Securing clients who represent the range of potential clients who might be seen by professional counselors is a problem area. Some clinics recruit clients from student populations with incentives for their participation. Should these students be treated as laboratory actors or counseling clients? If the students are screened to ensure they have legitimate concerns to discuss with their counselors, does their status change? How aggressively should a clinic subsidized by a counselor education program recruit clients in competition with private practitioners and fee-for-service clinics in the community? If counselor education students are assigned as counselors immediately after completing their laboratory-training experiences, should clients be told their counselors are at the beginning stages of a graduate program? We should note a concern in the medical profession about representing medical students as "doctors" (VandeCreek & Harrar, 1988). The reasonable desire of the counselor education faculty members to limit client concerns to those for which the students have developed competence might conflict with a desire to have the clinic model service for the full range of issues with which professional counselors deal. If the clinic is to deal with the full range of potential client problems, it would need to be staffed by professional counselors and advanced students, in addition to students at the beginning stage of their education as counselors.

Assignment of Clients to Counselors

Once the counseling clinic has a pool of potential clients, the dilemmas continue. Should clients be assigned to counselors on the basis of the counselors' needs for experience or on the basis of the counselor most likely to assist the client? If the clinic has a waiting list for services or limited availability of reduced or no-fee services, should clients be served as they appear on the list or on the basis of their presenting concern? Is providing expedited services to clients who present problems that match students' needs for experience proper or ethical? How should the clients who are counseled by counselor education faculty or by full-time clinic staff be selected?

Client Autonomy

What privileges, if any, does a client who seeks services from a counseling clinic operated by a counselor education program forfeit? For example, what about potential clients who refuse to be audio- or videotaped? Likewise, how do we deal with clients who have special requests? For example, how do we handle requests for a counselor of a particular gender, age, race, religion, and experience, which were among the special requests reported? Does a client who is paying have more rights to selection of a counselor than does the client who is not paying for services?

The Counseling Process

Counselor education programs operate on an academic schedule, but client needs do not follow semesters and academic break patterns. Even more troubling is the idea that if students are to receive most of their clinical experience in off-campus settings, they will have only limited availability for work in an on-campus clinic. Even if the operational concept of brief counseling were adopted by the clinic, students who were enrolled for a semester-long practicum could only accept clients when there was enough time remaining in the academic term to complete the counseling. A counselor education faculty cannot ask or demand of students who enroll for practicum or internship experiences in a program clinic to sacrifice other aspects of their program to allow the clinic to function continuously. The problem of time demand on students is more severe when the program assigns students for experiences that require travel to or residence at an off-campus site. Many programs that operate on an academic-semester system have month-long breaks between the first and second semester. The problem of faculty supervision for students during periods when academic faculty are not under contract is both an administrative and ethical issue. Counselor educators will have little success finding a counseling theory or approach that would justify interruption of counseling services to fit an academic schedule.

Community and Professional Relationships

The counselor education counseling clinic does not operate in a counseling-services vacuum. There are community agencies and, in most locales, licensed professional counselors who provide counseling services. Those agencies and counselors are the individuals who provide practicum and internship opportunities for students from the program. Should a counselor education counseling clinic accept only clients who have no resources to pay, or should it compete with the same professionals who support the program? If the counselor education clinic does not serve a full range of clients, should referrals be made to those who accept practicum students and interns, or should all professionals receive referrals? How should the clinic deal with referrals from area professionals when clients have exhausted their personal or insurance financial resources? What about potential clients who are referred for services that cannot be charged to third-party payers? Ethical and professional concerns were raised by one counselor education clinic that receives referrals from therapists who want to provide reimbursable therapy but ask the clinic to provide coordinated career counseling. How should a publicly supported institution refer to colleagues in private practice if the supervisor has an opinion of the quality of services offered by private practitioners who have asked for referrals from the clinic? Should private practitioners who take interns, have sliding fees, and are professionally active be favored?

Supervision

The continuing question in supervision literature is whether supervision should be focused on counselor growth or client progress. A similar question could be asked about clinics. The supervision question is answered unequivocally when the problem is harm to the client. For example, Cormier and Bernard (1982) concluded that, although "one goal of providing supervised practice is to produce more effective counselors, the most important goal is to protect the welfare of clients" (p. 489). The ACES Supervision Interest Network (1990) Standards for Counseling Supervisors (also ACES Draft, 1990) place the responsibility of the supervisor to the client above that to the supervisee. Despite the clear obligation to prevent harm to the client, there may be a contest between best service to the client and optimum training for the counselor education student in all phases of clinical instruction, particularly when the setting is a clinic operated by a counselor education program. However, the supervision concept of preventing harm cannot be easily translated into policies for a clinic. An institutional administrator will likely state that the only reason to provide the support necessary to operate a clinic is to provide student training. The client service provided is viewed as a fringe benefit of the training. Counseling clinics are different from teaching hospitals that have an acknowledged patient care and research mission in addition to their mission to train medical personnel. These issues and questions are all ingredients of this basic dilemma. The answers are easy at the extremes, but difficult when the issues are at the margins of professionally appropriate and ethical behavior. When does the institutional and professional responsibility of the counselor educator dictate that the counselor's autonomy, confidence, and potential for growth are sacrificed to protect the client? All would agree that the determining factor is harm, but there is no clear guidance when the issue is not so clear as harm to the client but is counseling service that is "less than the best."

Summary

The literature of counseling is clear that the foremost responsibility of the supervisor of the counseling trainee is to protect clients from harm. The literature is not so clear on dilemmas created when a counselor education program operates a counseling clinic. There are conflicts between the obligation of the counselor education program to provide opportunities for development for student counselors and the obligation to provide services to clients of a clinic that should be operated in an exemplary fashion. The dilemmas resulting from the conflicting obligations can be resolved only by balancing the competing demands of administrative, ethical, legal, and professional obligations to clients of the counselor education clinic with the obligation of the counselor education program to all students to develop counseling skills.

Implications

1. The CACREP standards should address the role of a counseling laboratory in the operation of an accredited program. The standards should clearly distinguish between requirements for a physical facility and requirements for a counseling clinic operated as part of a program.
2. The literature that addresses issues related to the supervision of counseling should be expanded to include consideration of the dilemmas faced by counselor educators who are charged with the operation of clinics. The issues should be considered and debated by those who study ethics and supervision and those who face the practical issues of training and clinic operation.
3. Counselor education faculties should define the role of clinics operated by their program and establish policies for the clinic. Policymaking should not be left to the faculty member assigned to direct the clinic; the clinic should be operated by the entire program faculty.
4. The administration of the institution that houses the clinic should be involved in the development of clinic policies and procedures. The institutional policies should be developed to acknowledge the primary obligation of the clinic for client welfare.
5. Counselor educators must consider the difficult issue of when "less than the best possible service" should be considered as potential harm to the client. Discussion of this issue is missing in the literature of counseling supervision and is necessary for a counselor education program to operate a clinic.

References

American Counseling Association [Formerly American Association for Counseling and Development]. (1988). *Ethical standards.* Alexandria, VA: Author.

Association for Counselor Education and Supervision. (1990). Ethical standards for counseling supervisors (Draft). *ACES Spectrum, 50*(3), 12–15.

Association for Counselor Education and Supervision, Supervision Interest Network. (1990). Standards for counseling supervisors. *Journal of Counseling and Development, 69,* 30–32.

Borders, L. D., & Leddick, G. R. (1987). *Handbook of counseling supervision.* Alexandria, VA: American Association for Counseling and Development.

Cormier, L. S., & Bernard, J. M. (1982). Ethical and legal responsibilities of clinical supervisors. *Personnel and Guidance Journal, 60,* 486–491.

Ethical principles of psychologists and code of conduct. (1992, December). *American Psychologist, 47,* 1597–1611.

VandeCreek, L., & Harrar, W. (1988). The legal liability of supervisors. *The Psychotherapy Bulletin, 23*(3), 13–16.

CHAPTER 11

REACTION: LEGAL AND ETHICAL ISSUES IN CLINICS

Brooke B. Collison

Pate and Remley did an excellent job of defining issues that must be addressed by counselor education programs involved in on-campus clinical-training laboratories. My initial reaction to their comprehensive list of potential impediments is to withdraw from any consideration of operating a clinic. Fortunately, they have raised the questions—as Pate says, "more questions than answers"—in such a way that a faculty group could use the two chapters as a comprehensive discussion outline before leaping into the seemingly overwhelming world of clinic operation.

Remley's comments reflect his professional background—that of counselor educator and attorney, as well as his position as executive director of American Counseling Association (ACA) where ethics violations are processed. His comments, although grounded in the law, do not seem to have that usual restrictiveness that I associate with legal statements. I was pleased to note his statement that it is impossible to eliminate all risk from our professional practice—that we, in fact, work to "manage the risk." I was also pleased to note his statement that it is important to obtain liability coverage that permits defense of the charges that may come as a regular part of doing business. Remley's point is that to practice totally devoid of risk would be to practice in so conservative and sterile a fashion that it would probably not be effective counseling. This is not to give license to rampant experimentation, however, and Remley makes the strong point that knowledge of the professional literature and the ethical guidelines is what frames professional practice.

In his methodically thorough thinking, Pate has raised more questions than many persons would be comfortable trying to answer. In doing so, he has placed a framework on counseling clinics that combines the education function with the treatment responsibility in a delicate balance considering client, counselor in training, clinic, institution, and the profession. I strongly urge counselor educators to use the Pate questions as an outline for discussions.

I suppose that I was asked to comment on these two chapters because of my long association with professional liability insurance through membership and chairmanship of the ACA Insurance Trust. In that capacity, I had occasion to see the kinds of claims that were brought against counselors. Fortunately, one of the low-frequency claims categories is against graduate students in counseling. Let us hope that reflects the fact that they are practicing under good supervision consistent with current knowledge of the profession.

I do raise one additional question that Pate and Remley did not address: Clinics imply supervision. What are the supervisory responsibilities with regard to liability and exposure to risk that accrue in an on-campus clinical-training facility? (Incidentally, these same issues could be rewritten with the word *off-campus* inserted in front of *clinical-training facility*, and the discussion could go on with even more intensity—a condition that many counselor education institutions face with part-time and off-campus students or in any off-campus internship.) The question I raise requires discussion of "how much" and "what" do supervisors see? In addition, who selects what the supervisor sees? If the supervisor sees only the good work of a counselor in training, is the supervisor responsible (e.g., liable) for the bad work that he or she does not see?

In my opinion, which I believe to be consistent with the viewpoints of both Remley and Pate, the supervisor is responsible for all work of the supervised counselor in training, even though he or she has not seen but a small part of it. This calls into question the issue of "sampling supervision." How much is enough? Standards are one way to answer this question: The Council for the Accreditation of Counseling and Related Educational Programs (CACREP) standards have set supervision ratios for practica and internship—both for individual and group supervision. Can the counseling-clinic director be assured that if a supervisor sees one tenth of a student's work that he or she has seen enough? Would it be possible for a student to present excellent and ethical work in his or her one-tenth sample and be totally reprehensible in some or all of his or her other nine tenths?

When I raised this question during the Association for Counselor Education and Supervision (ACES) think tank, one participant in the room asked, "Do you mean that I must watch every hour of my supervisee's work on a one-to-one ratio?" If one is to totally eliminate risk, then the answer is "yes." Counseling is not a risk-free profession, however, and the answer actually rests in the degree of comfort that the supervisor has about the work that he or she sees (or does not see) for the counselor in training. My guess is that the CACREP ratios are ones that have been worked out on an "it-seems-to-reason" rationale, and perhaps by a reasonable administrative staffing formula pattern. The more logical and developmental response would be that supervision ratios would be developed on a descending scale of time requirements across the internship or training experience. I would hope that one product of this book is that those ratios could be reexamined and that guidelines could be developed for setting supervision time requirements that have a more rational foundation.

These two chapters were great to read. They raised more questions than answers, but they guided my discussion with my own colleagues. I am sure the final result will be more professionally sound counselor education clinical-training laboratories.

PART IV

ON-CAMPUS ENTRY-LEVEL CLINICAL TRAINING

CHAPTER 12

ON-CAMPUS PRACTICUM: A MAJOR INVESTMENT IN EXCELLENCE

Allan Dye

Shortly after being assigned to direct an on-campus counseling clinic, Jane Myers started asking around among colleagues from other campuses: Does your counselor education program conduct its own clinic? How is it organized and operated, and by whom? In asking these and related questions, she managed to strike a spectacularly rich vein of ignorance about such clinics that penetrates the counselor-education mountain from base to pinnacle. With her colleague, Alfred Smith, she has taken several steps to begin the mining and refining process, including literature review, research, creation of the new Association for Counselor Education and Supervision (ACES) Interest Network for Directors of Clinical Training and Clinics, and the think tank at the 1992 ACES National Conference. In so doing, she has performed a valuable service for counselor education by calling attention to core procedures by which counseling methods and techniques are first taught. As amazing as it seems, there had been virtually no research or professional exchange on the topic of training clinics in counselor education until Myers and Smith got to work in 1992.

A review of the chapters in this book quickly reveals that, although nearly all counselor education programs offer a *practicum* and an *internship*, the terms describe activities that are sometimes markedly different from one campus to another. The semantic confusion related to internship description is no doubt addressed elsewhere in this book. Hence, for present purposes, the focus is on the term *practicum*. It seems fair to say that there is no standard, operational definition of the term. The Council for Accreditation of Counseling and Related Educational Programs

(CACREP) description is specific with respect to: (a) total amount of supervised experience (100 hours), (b) hours of contact (40), (c) amount of individual supervision (1 hour per week), and (d) amount of group supervision (1½ hours per week). However, these standards do not specify where the practicum is to be conducted, who the clientele shall be, nor who the instructor or supervisor shall be (Council for the Accreditation of Counseling and Related Educational Programs, 1988). The standards provide explicit quantitative criteria and identify basic components of a practicum from which an operational description may be inferred, but the lack of specificity regarding location, clientele, and instructional method allow for vast differences between programs. Further complicating the issue is the fact that many programs have not been accredited by CACREP, nor do their practices conform to CACREP standards.

In discussing with counselor educators from across the country how the counseling practicum is conducted, it becomes clear that (a) it is done both on campus and off; (b) faculty are actively involved in some programs, but not in others; (c) in some practica all sessions are simulations in which students serve as clients for one another, whereas in other settings all clientele are bona fide users of the clinic or agency; and (d) supervision is provided by a myriad of arrangements involving faculty, doctoral students, peers, and qualified and nonqualified agency personnel.

In this chapter, *practicum* is used to describe a course that requires students to serve as counselors for at least 100 hours of supervised practice (including 40 hours of direct client contact) in an on-campus counseling facility that provides counseling services to individuals other than students in the counselor education program. The facility can be operated by the counselor education program for the specific purpose of providing a practicum and internship site, or it can be operated as a student/community service by the dean of students or similar authority with provision for a built in practicum program. Faculty supervision includes a weekly group session and regular, periodic individual conferences. In the absence of intense, personal instruction and supervision by a faculty member as prescribed by CACREP (no more than five students as a one-course assignment), additional supervision is provided by other qualified personnel such as doctoral students or counseling practitioners who wish to acquire experience as supervisors. The counseling practicum course is taken prior to a counseling internship and includes significantly more instruction and supervision.

The issue is this: Shall the counselor education program conduct the counseling practicum on campus, either in its own facility or using the facility of another campus counseling service, or shall the practicum be conducted off campus using the facilities, clientele, and supervisory assistance of cooperating agencies, services, and schools?

Advantages of an On-Campus Practicum

The position taken herein is that the counseling practicum serves as the keystone in the total preparation program arch. No other single experience (a) incorporates as much of the curriculum, (b) provides as well for students' professional growth, (c) makes use of the faculty's knowledge and skill, or (d) demonstrates the counselor education program's viability.

Advantages for Counselor Education Students

Students are given an opportunity to practice within well-defined, limited circumstances. That is, student counselors know the characteristics and typical presenting concerns of clientele, there is a well-equipped facility in which to practice, the distractions from the counseling task are few, and it is less likely that they will be called on to provide services for which they are not at all qualified.

Students have the luxury of immediate access to qualified instruction and consultation from individuals with whom they are acquainted. Convenience is an important feature; facilities and clients are provided, and the time for counseling sessions, peer feedback, and supervision has been predetermined. Relatively small amounts of time and energy must be devoted to logistical matters. Feedback, a primary ingredient in learning, is available from peers, advanced students, instructors, and from reviewing video- and audiotapes of one's own sessions. Vicarious learning occurs by observing and consulting with others who are simultaneously engaged in the same learning experience.

The on-campus practicum provides an opportunity to experience active, task-focused supervision. That is, supervisors in this setting are less distracted than might be possible in an agency or school setting, thus they are able to concentrate more fully on the counselor's work and on supervision processes. When both student counselors and their supervisors are provided with an environment designed specifically for practice and training, there is a corresponding increase in the quality of counseling, learning, and supervision.

Students who complete a rigorous on-campus practicum consistently report that they have rarely been as fully challenged as when they have been held accountable to their clients, the clinic facility, the graduate program, and their own expectations regarding effective performance. Some report having learned more about themselves, human nature, and interpersonal influence processes than in any other educational or employment experience.

Advantages for the Graduate Program

An on-campus practicum operation is a laboratory for studying the teaching and learning of knowledge and competencies relative to counseling and counselor supervision. Everyone involved is both student and teacher. In addition, the laboratory can be a source of data for faculty and student research. Such an environment is highly consistent with the goals of graduate education.

An on-campus practicum that includes (a) live observation, (b) in situ supervision, (c) frequent feedback, and (d) consultation sessions enables the teaching and learning of complex skills and concepts. These outcomes can be achieved in other settings, of course, but not as efficiently and perhaps not as thoroughly.

An invaluable by-product of an on-campus practicum is the simultaneous creation of a supervision opportunity for advanced students or local practitioners who wish to acquire competency in supervision. In the majority of instances cited in this book (see part V), supervision of this type is described as a practicum in supervision for doctoral students in counselor education. However, it may well be that other students are qualified for such training, including advanced master's students and recent graduates. Students serving as supervisors must also be trained and supervised, of course. Some counselor educators are challenged and invigorated by this prospect; others turn away. In any case, the advantages of having additional supervisory assistance must be weighed against the cost of administering such a structure.

More easily than by any other arrangement, the on-campus practicum enables faculty to demonstrate their knowledge and skills as counselors and supervisors. A common practice in some on-campus facilities is the observing by students of a faculty member serving as counselor in exchange for the client's permission to allow observation of sessions. It may also be possible for a supervising faculty member to serve as a co-counselor with a student on a continuing basis or periodically as appropriate. In terms of supervision competency, more is called for when the faculty member is present during and immediately following a counselor–client interaction than when supervision occurs only later, without first-hand awareness but with the dubious advantage of hindsight based on others' recollections. In other words, supervising in the moment requires attending to the counselor in the moment, in addition to whatever teaching and consultation may be appropriate. Immediacy makes the difference.

An on-campus practicum provides a service to clients and the constituencies they represent. The value of the service can be reported in tangible terms of hours, number of sessions, number of individuals served, and the like. The college or university benefits by acquiring visible evidence of service to the community.

Finally, an on-campus practicum creates a liaison with (a) community mental health agencies, (b) mental health practitioners, and (c) a variety of referral sources. Being well connected in this way can be of value when (a) seeking consultation relative to curriculum revision, (b) locating sites for internship assignments, and (c) identifying those who have expertise in various mental health specializations.

Advantages for Clients

Directors of on-campus practica who have contributed to this book report that their counseling services are provided without fee, for a one-time nominal fee, or on a sliding-fee basis according to financial means. The availability of free or low-cost service is a significant advantage for many clients. A standard condition is that clients permit observation and audio/video recording of sessions.

Some clients have reported that it is easier to make contact, get an appointment, and be seen in a campus facility than in a local mental health center. In addition, they feel more comfortable in a campus environment than in either a mental health center or private-practice setting.

Career assessment and counseling are usually offered in on-campus counseling services, but are not always available from mental health facilities. In smaller cities and rural areas, it is sometimes difficult to find qualified career counselors in private practice. Educational/life/career assessment and counseling with nonstudent adults constitutes a significant category of activity in many clinics.

Costs and Disadvantages

An initial challenge in establishing a counseling clinic is acquiring space. If the clinic is to be part of a new building, it is necessary to convince a great many people that the space allocation can be justified in both educational and economic terms. More often than not, however, counseling clinics become housed in space formerly occupied by someone else who used the facility for some other purpose. The same arguments must be made as with the building of a new facility. In addition, there is also the need to justify a clinic as more necessary, desirable, or mission serving than some other program. The cost of furnishing and equipping a clinic can be imposing, particularly if there is to be full provision for live observation and electronic recording. The cost varies depending on: (a) the quantity of furniture and monitoring equipment to be purchased, (b) the level of sophistication desired for video/audio recording, and (c) the quality of furniture and other accoutrements (carpeting, wall decorations, etc.) to be used.

Another formidable and perpetual challenge in operating an on-campus counseling clinic is the availability of clientele whose circumstances and personal characteristics are reasonably well matched to the knowledge and competencies of the counselors, supervisors, and supervising faculty who perform and oversee the counseling activity. If clients' requests present too little challenge for the use of counseling skills (requests for information, routine advising, instruction in study habits, etc.), nothing much can be gained. Clients who are in crisis, are significantly impaired in some way, or require medical consultation are poor candidates for the sort of counseling to be performed during a first or second practicum. Again, very little purpose is served. Establishing and sustaining a productive referral network requires frequent communication with cooperating agencies, institutions, and individuals in the community. Moreover, there must be provision for screening and referring to various other sources of assistance those who cannot be well served at the clinic.

The issue of liability should be explored with the institution's legal counsel to determine that faculty, staff, and students are protected. The people who provide service directly to the public are well advised to carry their own liability insurance in addition to coverage provided by the institution.

A comprehensive system for recording and reporting would include such records as: (a) client personal data forms, (b) intake reports, (c) interview notes, (d) supervisor records, (e) assessment results, (f) exit/

final reports, (g) correspondence with other professionals, (h) referral records, and (i) the like. Some counselor education clinics report using a computer for recording and storing these data, whereas others continue to rely on hard copy. Both systems require that users be trained, that all records and reports be edited for accuracy and appropriateness, that client confidentiality be preserved, and that records be stored securely while at the same time being accessible to those who use them. Professional and ethical standards require that records such as these be kept. Experience has demonstrated that this necessary function is best performed by support personnel employed for this purpose—that it is unrealistic to believe that instructors or student supervisors can maintain records in a satisfactory, reliable manner while also performing their vital roles as teachers, trainers, supervisors, and consultants.

A final consideration is physical accessibility: (a) location within the community, (b) availability of public transportation, (c) availability of parking for nonstudent clients during clinic hours, (d) wheelchair accessibility, and (e) accommodations for visually and hearing-impaired persons. This factor can have a major influence on the rate of nonreturning and no-show clients, even when service is provided at nominal cost. Clinic directors have been known to complain, "Our clients will avail themselves of our generosity only when we make it extremely convenient for them to do so!"

Instructional Deterrents

There are several important ways in which the nature of a graduate educational enterprise can be at some degree of variance with a program of training and service. The most conspicuous example is that the conventional academic reward system promotes, literally and figuratively, the practicing of a monastic life consisting of solitary research and writing, as free as possible from the wasteful encumbrances associated with students and teaching. On the other hand, a teaching clinic requires high levels of faculty participation in tutorial, supervisory, and consultative activity. When these value systems collide, there are casualties.

Logistics and communications constitute a major challenge. A clinic staff might include one or more of the following: (a) secretary/receptionist, (b) administrator, (c) student counselor, (d) student supervisor, and (e) supervising faculty member. Each of these individuals must be responsible for information about clients that is exchanged with each of the others using confidentiality precautions. Arrangements must be made and communicated among the staff regarding appointments for counseling, assessment, supervision, staff meetings, and the like. Records must be prepared, edited, circulated to all concerned, and stored. These and other functions are performed by individuals who engage in clinic and practicum activities on only a part-time basis; all have other obligations in other locations. Consequently, great pains must be taken to establish and maintain clear, open, and frequent communication between participants.

Operating a clinic introduces a clinical versus nonclinical dimension to the composition of the department's faculty. It is likely that some faculty may enjoy and prefer clinical instruction, whereas others either shun such duty or are ineffective. A common result is that nonclinically engaged faculty spend less time with students, thus enabling them, theoretically, to devote more time to scholarship and research. Those who provide clinical instruction then assert that they not only are obliged to spend more time with students, but that in so doing they are placed at a disadvantage with respect to the institution's reward system that does not incorporate clinical instruction.

The supervision factor pervades virtually every aspect of a clinic's operation. Thus, it must be addressed from educational and financial points of view and within the framework of the faculty's qualifications and priorities. The basic question is this: How will students be supervised? CACREP standards for practicum instruction specify a student-to-faculty ratio of 5:1. This is expensive arithmetic. The immediate alternative is to enlist additional, less costly supervisory personnel. Who? How and by whom are these individuals to be trained? Who shall supervise them as they assist with the practicum? Although the use of nonfaculty may be necessary, an entirely new set of philosophical, academic, and operational factors must be addressed.

Summary

Recent conversations initiated among ACES members suggest that very little information has been collected about the operation of on-campus counseling clinics by counselor education programs throughout the country. Several such clinics are known to exist, some for many years, but their former and current directors have apparently not communicated with one another. However, it seems clear that most programs do not have such a clinic, and that practicum activity more frequently occurs at off-campus locations. There appears to be great variation in how the practicum is conducted with respect to location, clientele, instructional methods, and supervision arrangements. There is more than form at stake here. We are also asking, who is doing the training and what is being taught?

An on-campus clinic offers advantages to (a) counselor education students, (b) counselor education programs, and (c) clients. A clinic offers students the opportunity to learn in a facility that has been staffed and equipped for the specific purpose of providing an enriched learning experience. Features include: (a) access to in situ supervision and consultation, (b) opportunity to be observed and to observe others, (c) a pool of appropriately qualified clients with whom to work, (d) a convenient location, and (e) the luxury of counseling in an environment that is relatively free of distractions and other responsibilities.

A clinic serves as a focal point for the counselor education program and is a laboratory for studying the teaching and learning of knowledge and competencies relative to counseling and counselor supervision. Faculty are more actively involved in the teaching of complex skills and concepts and are able to make effective use of their competencies in counseling and supervising. A clinic operation inevitably expands the program's scope to include the training of supervisors who may be doctoral students, advanced master's students, recent graduates, or volunteers from local agencies and schools who wish to develop competencies in supervision. A clinic provides service to campus and local constituents; in so doing, relationships are formed with community mental health agencies, practitioners, and a variety of referral sources.

Among the costs and disadvantages of operating a clinic are the acquiring and maintaining of space, equipment, and furnishings. The processes of attracting and screening prospective clientele require perpetual diligence, and it is necessary to maintain relationships with several referral sources. The matter of liability must be addressed thoroughly. Recording and reporting account for significant portions of all staff members' time in the clinic; these functions must be performed with meticulous attention to accuracy and confidentiality. If the clinic is open to the public, it becomes necessary to provide for convenient access.

From a purely instructional point of view, there are several deterrents to operating a clinic. Most prominent is that the nature of didactic education is quite different from that of clinical training. Not only is the institution sometimes inhospitable, but there can be fallout from the academician versus clinician preferences among the counselor education faculty. A clinic operation compounds the counselor education program's organizational structure and creates the need for a highly effective, comprehensive communication system among faculty, students, and staff.

Implications

1. On-campus training is clearly superior to an off-campus, nonobservable practicum experience in preparing counselors who are knowledgeable, skillful, and confident.
2. Viewed from a learning theory perspective, the intensive laboratory form of practicum offers several significant advantages, most of which accrue from the observation and supervision dimensions.
3. There are several obstacles to operating a clinic for practicum purposes. Among these are the costs of establishing and maintaining the physical facility and support staff, requiring faculty to divert their energies from scholarship and research to clinical instruction, and performing an array of tasks inherent in providing service to the public.
4. In view of the costs and various accommodations that are necessary for the successful operation of an on-campus clinic, the decision to establish or maintain an existing facility should have universal support, if possible, including the department faculty and the institution's administrators at all levels.

References

Council for Accreditation of Counseling and Related Educational Programs. (1988). *Accreditation procedures manual and application.* Alexandria, VA: Author.

CHAPTER 13

PREPARING COUNSELORS TO WORK WITH TODAY'S CLINIC CLIENTS

Susan Allstetter Neufeldt

The client population seen in university training clinics has changed radically in the past 20 years, moving from a preponderance of fairly normal developmental concerns, including academic difficulty and uncomplicated communication problems, to more severe disorders. Examples of presenting problems seen in the author's clinic, the Ray E. Hosford Clinic at the University of California at Santa Barbara (UCSB), are bulimia, borderline personality disorder, depression, family conflict, and gang activities. The population of the author's clinic, which serves the community on a sliding-scale basis, reflects similar changes across the country. Kramer (1983) noted a "rising pandemic of mental disorders and associated chronic diseases and disabling conditions" (p. 115), which is complicated by difficult economic conditions, and a more mobile society, leaving both individuals and families without needed social support and resources for medical and mental health care. These clients overwhelm teaching facilities, as well as the schools (Hooks, Mayes, & Volkmar, 1988; Links, 1983), college counseling centers (Harris & Kranz, 1991), student health services, and community agencies, where many counseling students work after graduation.

Basic helping skills no longer suffice to prepare students to work with their first clients in a campus-based clinic. For some time now, counselor educators in the graduate program at the author's university have said, "Oh, this is the wrong client for our students; let's wait until we get a developmental case." Slowly, the faculty supervisors have come to believe that the client who presents in this clinic is the client with whom the students must learn to work.

Changes in Clinic Procedures

To meet the needs of both the student and the client population, the author's clinic has instituted a number of changes in both clinic procedures and the initial practicum course. First, supervision has been intensified.

The training clinic has been remodeled and includes video cameras in each room, with a central bank of recorders in a video control room. All counseling sessions are videotaped and may be viewed live by a supervisor from the control room or from an adjacent classroom. During the first 2 years of training, each counselor is supervised weekly either directly by a licensed, experienced faculty member, or by an advanced doctoral student supervisor who has completed a course in supervision theory and is enrolled in a supervision practicum under the careful supervision of the clinic director. Student supervisors are provided with a supervision manual (Neufeldt, Iversen, & Juntunen, 1993), and their supervision sessions are videotaped so that the clinic director can monitor both supervision and the cases of the beginning students.

Second, a series of intake procedures has been developed. All potential clients receive a packet of information about the clinic and some basic questionnaires to fill out and bring to the first session. Individual adults fill out individual life histories, adolescents fill out their own life-history forms, and adults fill out family-background questionnaires when an entire family is involved. When clients come to an intake, they are prepared to spend 2–3 hours with the intake counselor (or counselors, in the case of a couple or family) talking about their concerns and responding to additional assessments appropriate to their needs. Career inventories are given to career-counseling clients, a basic symptom checklist and a brief computerized structured diagnostic instrument to individuals with personal concerns, a standard couples-adjustment scale to couples, and a standardized family scale to families. This extensive intake allows for treatment planning to be initiated at the beginning of counseling and for assignment of cases to appropriate student counselors.

Changes in First-Year Practicum

The curriculum for the beginning practicum has been substantially changed in response to client needs. An extensive didactic component is paired with a practical component to prepare students to deal effectively with the cases they are likely to see. This process makes them more helpful to their clients. In addition, this preparation helps to avoid some of the difficulties and disappointments students may experience with clients, and enables them to cope with problems in a context that minimizes their sense of failure and personal inadequacy when clients do not progress as planned.

The UCSB graduate counseling program has a commitment to training counselors to be responsive to cross-cultural influences. As shown by Sue and Sue (1990), clients from different cultures often have differing expectations of counseling. To respond respectfully to those differences and to use interventions that are culturally appropriate, counselors must be culturally sensitive. Although many of the specifics of different cultures are taught in required coursework in the program, an endeavor is made to apply cross-cultural principles in the practicum setting.

Students' first practicum follows their initial academic term, in which they are exposed to basic counseling theory and issues of diversity in counseling. The practicum extends for two academic quarters, and each quarter's work has a focus. The focus of the initial quarter is relationship building. Students are asked to read Gelso and Carter's (1985) seminal work on the counseling relationship. Although much of it is difficult to assimilate at this stage of their training, it provides a framework for their work and an underlying theme throughout the quarter.

In the context of relationship building, the practicum begins by teaching students to: (a) make appointments, (b) open and close sessions, (c) collect fees, and (d) establish firm boundaries with clients. Boundary setting is a particularly difficult skill for beginning counselors to learn when they just want to be accepted by clients and present a helpful presence, but it has proved critical in building relationships of trust. Many difficulties and failure experiences can be avoided by teaching this skill early on in the learning process. Then basic listening skills are taught, as well as the use of confrontation, interpretation, and summarization. This is followed with specific training in basic interviewing skills with children.

Students learn, in a step-by-step procedure, how to conduct intake interviews with individuals and families, and they are prepared for the crisis situations that can sometimes occur at the first interview. Such crisis training includes suicide assessment, child and elder abuse assessment and reporting, and procedures for getting assistance from the on-duty supervisor in the face of an abusive or acting-out client. Although students may not encounter any of these situations in their first year of training, they are prepared for them.

In addition to the didactic class, which meets for several hours each week, students spend 3 hours a week with a student supervisor and one or two colleagues from the beginning practicum. They practice the skills they are being taught in supervision and, outside of class time, conduct role-plays with fellow students that are videotaped and critiqued at the next supervision session. They also present their videotapes once or twice during the quarter in the larger practicum class with the course instructor. About halfway through the quarter, each practicum student is assigned to conduct three sessions with undergraduate students who are taking a course in counseling skills and "want to experience counseling." The undergraduates are screened out of the experience if they are already in counseling with a professional, and they are encouraged only to raise issues appropriate to the three-session format, such as roommate issues or academic problems. On the whole, this provides a good inital experience for student counselors. Because no screening is perfect, counselors are sometimes faced with unexpected issues such as sexual abuse or eating disorders. In these instances, arrangements are made for clients to receive services at the university counseling center on a longer term basis. By the end of the quarter, students begin to conduct their first intake interviews, usually with an advanced student's assistance.

The second quarter focuses on case conceptualization and treatment planning. Students are presented with a model of case conceptualization (see Appendix F; Beutler & Clarkin, 1990; Mahoney, 1991; Persons, Curtis, & Silberschatz, 1992) that allows them to integrate interview and assessment information to determine the nature of the problem and an initial contract with the client. Goal setting is taught here, and students are encouraged to select appropriate change strategies and work with the client to determine the outcomes that would constitute successful counseling. Like the Gelso and Carter (1985) article, much of this model is initially beyond their understanding; but as the quarter progresses, they begin to fit their experiences into this framework.

With the framework in mind, the didactic portion of the course addresses a number of problems commonly presented by clients. Topics discussed include strategies for providing assertiveness training and career planning for developmental clients, and for treating depression in adults and adolescents, anxiety in adults and children, and posttraumatic stress disorder. In each instance, at least two theoretical approaches to treatment are presented. Although this is often more than a student can assimilate and use in one quarter, it provides the student with a jumping-off place in dealing with clients as well as resources to pursue further.

During the second quarter, students (a) complete their initial intake interviews, (b) conduct a second series of three-session counseling with undergraduate volunteer clients, and (c) begin working with their first community clients. Supervision is conducted by the student supervisors in alternating group and individual sessions, as well as by the faculty instuctor in the larger class format. During this quarter, the faculty instructor also watches one or more entire sessions conducted by each student and meets with the student after the session to provide immediate feedback.

Preliminary Results and Summary

Practicum students report feeling overwhelmed, anxious, excited, and stimulated by the course. At the end of the first year with the new curriculum, a student said, to the author's amazement, "This course was wonderful. We really had to work hard, but we learned a lot in a very supportive atmosphere." That feedback was encouraging and was echoed in anonymously submitted course evaluations. These students were better prepared at the end of this intensive training experience than students previously trained in the clinic.

By examining the presenting problems of clients in the training clinic, as well as the demographic patterns in the population at large, it becomes apparent that training of students has to change. In the Hosford clinic, students are prepared in their very first practicum experience to begin to work with difficult clients who present challenging problems. An attempt is made to graduate their experiences with clients, by having them role-play with one another at first, see undergraduate volunteers, then do intakes with community clients, and finally begin to do counseling with community clients. However, it is acknowledged that they are likely to encounter difficult situations, and every effort is made to prepare them to work with difficult clients effectively. In the process, students are prepared more realistically for the work that awaits them postgraduation.

Implications for Training

The experiences in the Ray E. Hosford Clinic discussed in this chapter have implications for training all across the country. The major implications are as follows:

1. Clients at all agency sites, from college counseling centers to mental health agencies and university training clinics, are presenting with increasingly large numbers of serious problems. Students will work with such clients both in training and on the job to a much greater extent than they have previously.
2. Previous training methods, which focused on basic counseling skills, will not adequately train students to deal with a more severe client population.
3. From the very beginning of their training, students need to learn to set and maintain firm boundaries, to manage crises, and, most importantly, to get immediate assistance from more experienced professionals.
4. It is important to facilitate the development of the counselor's professional self-esteem in the face of difficult client problems and inevitable treatment failures while continuing to train him or her to have more successes in clinical work.

References

Beutler, L. E., & Clarkin, J. B. (1990). *Systematic treatment selection.* New York: Brunner-Mazel.

Gelso, C. J., & Carter, J. (1985). The relationship in counseling and psychotherapy: Components, consequences, and theoretical antecedents. *The Counseling Psychologist, 13*(2), 155–243.

Harris, S. A., & Kranz, P. (1991). Small college counseling centers: Changing trends for a new decade. *Journal of College Student Psychotherapy, 5*(3), 81–89.

Hooks, M. Y., Mayes, L. C., & Volkmar, F. R. (1988). Psychiatric disorders among preschool children. *Journal of the American Academy of Child and Adolescent Psychiatry, 27*(5), 623–627.

Kramer, M. (1983). The increasing prevalence of mental disorders: A pandemic threat. *Psychiatric Quarterly, 55*, 115–243.

Links, P. S. (1983). Community surveys of the prevalence of childhood psychiatric disorders: A review. *Child Development, 54*, 531–548.

Mahoney, M. J. (1991). *Human change processes: The scientific foundations of psychotherapy.* New York: Basic Books.

Neufeldt, S. A., Iversen, J. N., & Juntunen, C. L. (1993). *Structured supervision for first practicum.* Unpublished manuscript, University of California at Santa Barbara.

Persons, J. B., Curtis, J. T., & Silberschatz, G. (1992). Psychodynamic and cognitive-behavioral formulations of a single case. *Psychotherapy, 28*(4), 608–617.

Sue, D. W., & Sue, D. (1990). *Counseling the culturally different: Theory and practice* (2nd ed.). New York: Wiley.

CHAPTER 14

REACTION: ON-CAMPUS PRACTICUM AND SUPERVISION

Peggy H. Smith

I am delighted the authors have addressed two different aspects of the on-campus training experience: (a) the advantages and disadvantages of such a program, and (b) a specific model of how to train beginning students. After I respond to their chapters, I comment on chapter 1 as well.

There is no doubt in my mind, as Dye noted, that an in-house training clinic is the best form of training for students. Counselor educators can control what students are learning and how they learn it. They can match their curriculum to their training experiences. They can provide for direct observation of, and immediate feedback on, the students' work.

Counselor educators can better monitor the quality of their supervision. Too often, "in the field," supervision becomes secondary, even among the best tried-and-true supervisors, to the other demands of their jobs in schools, clinics, and businesses. For example, hours set aside for supervision get eaten up in emergencies. Supervision is done "on the fly." Sometimes even space becomes an issue, and either the counseling or the supervision is done in the first available corner to be found.

Because the primary commitment of our faculty at San Francisco State University (SFSU) is to training, we can ensure that the in-house practicum experience embraces a comprehensive and intensive training component that is too often missing "in the field." Especially when a setting has only one or two trainees, mounting a training program is not cost-effective.

However, the drawbacks are also there. Primary among them is the ever-present threat, which has been acted out in part on my own campus: When funding is tight, the clinic is the first thing to go. The institutional commitment must constantly be massaged. The powerful figures in the administration must be convinced that nothing is going on "down there" that will put the campus "at risk." I include here not only issues of liability, but also such nefarious no-goodnik activities as convincing students to drop out, or supporting students who are complaining about professors, graduation requirements, or institutional red tape. Incidentally, these are the same issues of "dual loyalties" faced by any counselors within institutions.

Other issues, such as confidentiality, are to be handled carefully. For example, we excluded as potential clients anyone who was a student in the graduate program of counseling, and excluded as trainees anyone who had been seen by an SFSU counselor (because they acted as supervisors). It was also difficult, on occasion, to keep counseling department professors who were not involved with the clinic directly from wanting to "help out" in ways that jeopardized the confidentiality of the files or the appointment book, or from wanting to intervene directly in a case that, they knew from the classroom, was distressing a student counselor.

I was also very impressed by the training program outlined by Neufeldt. I especially like the extensive homework that is done by the client before the first meeting with the student counselor.

I would like to emphasize the importance of early training in handling emergencies. Most crucial here is the importance of *asking for help*. In almost every case in which an "uproar" has occurred in our clinic, it was because the trainee tried to fix a difficult clinical issue without immediately withdrawing to ask the on-site supervisor, who is always available for consultation, for assistance. When this consultation was done, 9 times out of 10 the trainee could handle the issue effectively without the necessity for the on-site supervisor's actually coming into the session.

In my mind, it is crucial to have this on-site supervision. (It is also a very good selling point to the nervous people "upstairs" if you are wanting to create an in-house training clinic on your campus.) Whenever our clinic was open, we had a licensed mental health professional in the building. Most times, this person was simply "on call." We emphasized to the trainees that, when the on-site supervisor was involved in another activity, such as a meeting, this supervisor would always respond to a request for a consultation on the spot.

I would also like to emphasize the importance of informed consent. As was the case in our clinic, when the primary purpose of the setting is training, it is important for clients to know this. We had a one-page informed consent form that every client had to sign before the first session began. This included information about (a) the purpose of the clinic, (b) the fact that supervisors and other trainees would be observing and listening to audiotapes (each session was taped), (c) the fact that cases would be discussed during training meetings, and (d) the limits of confidentiality imposed legally: suicide, homocide, abuse. Clients refusing to sign this form were referred to other settings.

We also found the level of pathology increasing since the clinic opened in 1983. I agree that the best approach to this is to teach the students that these will be the clients they see. Dealing with developmental issues is a luxury that our society, institutions, and insurance companies will no longer indulge. I believe the consequences of this are far reaching and tragic, but I do believe that this is the reality we face.

As a long-time supervisor, I would like to conclude my reactions to this presentation by reemphasizing the importance of teaching limits and boundaries to trainees. Inability to do this is probably the most common problem that I have with trainees. We get into this profession for a number of reasons, but one basic motivation is the "need to help." All too frequently, this need directly interferes with the trainees' ability to set limits and boundaries. We all "face" this potential training problem as professors and supervisors, but when you are working with an in-house training clinic, the difference is the trainees' inability to set limits and boundaries "in your face." Their client is literally at your door.

The Role of the Director

I referred earlier to chapter 1. One issue raised in that chapter, and discussed in detail in chapters 5–8, is that the role and position of the director in on-campus clinics is very complex. The pecking order of academic departments being what it is, it is crucial, for the long-term health of the clinic, that the director be a tenured full professor. If the academic department is not fully aware of, and fully supportive of, the training clinic, it will always be short changed when hard decisions have to be made about teaching assignments, release time, budget, and space. The best way to get this solid commitment is to have the clinic's day-to-day handling firmly entrenched in the more ossified echelons of the academic department. (I say that with all due respect to my senior colleagues.)

PART V

ON-CAMPUS TRAINING OF DOCTORAL-LEVEL SUPERVISORS

CHAPTER 15

TRAINING DOCTORAL STUDENT SUPERVISORS AT PURDUE UNIVERSITY

Allan Dye

Judging from the dates of important publications devoted to counselor supervision, it might appear that the training of doctoral-level supervisors has developed only recently. For example, the "Standards for Counseling Supervisors" were published in 1990 (American Association for Counseling and Development, 1990) and the "Curriculum Guide for Training Counseling Supervisors" appeared 1 year later (Borders et al., 1991). However, the training of doctoral-level supervisors has been going on for several decades. Doctoral students in counselor education have been participating as practicum supervisors since at least 1962—more than 30 years ago—when the author's assignment as a graduate assistant in the NDEA Institute at Purdue University that year was to assist in supervising an on-campus practicum. This was a common practice at several programs in the north-central region of the Association for Counselor Education and Supervision (ACES) and, no doubt, throughout the country, at least in programs having NDEA funds with which to employ graduate assistants. It seems ironic that the field of counselor education is just now turning attention to its own special training methods and programs after first developing standards, certification programs, and accrediting criteria for counselors and other related professionals.

Although doctoral-level training in supervision has been going on for many years, it appears that practitioners have not published descriptions of their methods nor have they devoted anything more than casual attention to the topic in regional and national conferences. The "Think

Tank on Counselor Education Laboratories" during the 1992 ACES National Conference provided a long overdue forum for exchanging straightforward descriptions of training programs, along with the opportunity to discuss problems, successes, and prospects.

This chapter provides an example of one approach to training doctoral-level supervisors. The system described here is offered neither as a perfect structure nor as a model for others to emulate. It is merely an account of how one counselor education program prepares doctoral supervisors. Perhaps this information will be useful to others who seek to initiate or revise their procedures and structures.

The Counselor Education Program and the Campus Setting for Practica

Before the supervision practicum can be described, it is necessary first to provide a brief explanation of the context. The counselor education program at Purdue University, entitled Counseling and Development Section, is part of the Department of Educational Studies in the School of Education. Three 60-semester-hour master's-level programs; Community/Agency, Student Affairs in Higher Education, and School Counseling; and a doctoral program in Counselor Education have been accredited by the Council for Accreditation of Counseling and Related Educational Programs (CACREP). In 1991, seven full-time and four part-time faculty members were engaged in teaching one or more graduate courses each. The program enrolls approximately 65 master's students and 35 doctoral students, in addition to approximately 10 nondegree-seeking students. The Counseling and Development Section operates the Purdue Counseling and Guidance Center to provide a clinical/laboratory setting for beginning and advanced counseling practica. The center is open to the public, and its clientele include: (a) adults from the surrounding community, (b) university students, and (c) students from area high schools. Counseling is done primarily with individual clients, but service is also provided to a small number of couples and families. Facilities are shared with the Psychological Services Center, a counseling service for university students only, which is operated by the dean of students. All counseling occurs in observable rooms, and all sessions are audio recorded. Video recording is available and is used when supervisors cannot be present. Clients are fully briefed regarding the observation and supervision practices; they are encouraged to ask questions or pursue any apprehension they may have, and then decide whether to permit observation and recording. Those who decline are assisted in locating alternative sources for counseling. The center's policy is that inexperienced counselors in training can provide service only when they are being supervised.

The Counseling and Guidance Center is staffed entirely by faculty, secretarial staff, and students from the Counseling and Development Section. A half-time graduate assistant is employed as a coordinator and is responsible for (a) maintaining the record system, (b) orienting new counselors to the center's procedures, (c) monitoring the assignment of clients to counselors, (d) assisting doctoral student supervisors by coordinating counselors' reports, and (e) fulfilling other miscellaneous administrative functions. The center's director is a faculty member from the Counseling and Development Section whose primary duties are to (a) ensure a steady supply of clientele, (b) oversee the intake procedure, (c) make client assignments or referrals, and (d) prepare periodic reports of service.

Counselors are students in either a first counseling practicum or an advanced counseling practicum who typically accumulate 40 or more hours of contact during a semester. Each counselor conducts 1–4 sessions per week. Each student in the first practicum is supervised by a doctoral student and by a faculty member; students in the advanced practicum are supervised only by a faculty member. Thus, it should be clear that the center is an integral part of the counselor education program and that, except for one half-time graduate assistant (the only salary item in the budget), all functions are performed by faculty, staff, and students who devote only part of their time to the center.

The Supervision Practicum

The Practicum in Counseling Supervision (supervision practicum) is the largest and most important event in a sequence of education and training activities, as is explained. The supervision practicum occurs as early in the student's doctoral program as his or her prior experience will permit, ordinarily in the second year.

Eligibility

To be eligible, a student must have successfully completed a beginning and advanced practicum, a prepracticum laboratory course in supervision, and have the practicum instructor's permission (i.e., completion of the prerequisites does not guarantee admission to the supervision practicum).

The instructor must exercise judgment in deciding whether students who meet the experience requirement are sufficiently mature and personally qualified to meet the leadership demands of the course. Students who apply but are not admitted are assisted in identifying additional education, training, or personal growth experiences that address their lack of readiness for the course. Students who have completed at least one advanced counseling practicum by that time have also completed approximately 60 or more hours of coursework and may also have acquired a significant amount of relevant practical experience that should enhance their qualifications. As a rule, students have previously served as laboratory instructors for a prepracticum laboratory course in counseling skills. This experience provides a preview of the student supervisor's teaching and relationship styles. It should also be observed that the study and practice of counseling supervision as a part of doctoral education is not a matter of teaching entirely new concepts and methods to naive learners. All students at this level have had considerable experience with teachers and teaching, supervisors and supervising, by whatever nomenclature may have been used. Consequently, the training of doctoral supervisors includes a great deal of reformulating and reconceptualizing prior experience.

The Prepracticum Laboratory

A prepracticum laboratory course in supervision is conducted twice per year. This 16-hour required lab is offered without credit or fee and is usually conducted either in two 8-hour sessions or four 4-hour sessions. The content and activities vary somewhat from one occasion to the next, but they always include: (a) the Discrimination Model (Bernard, 1979), (b) demonstration and practice of in situ (often called "live") supervision, (c) demonstration and practice of Interpersonal Process Recall (Kagan, 1980), and (d) discussion of ethicolegal dilemmas. Additional topics include the "Standards for Counseling Supervisors" (American Association for Counseling and Development, 1990), the "Curriculum Guide for Training Counseling Supervisors" (Borders et al., 1991), discussion of one's best and worst supervisors and how they behaved, the place of supervision in one's career objectives, and the like.

Practice Component

The supervision practicum consists of three components: (a) practice, (b) didactic, and (c) supervision/consultation. The practice component entails serving as a first-line supervisor of three (usually) master's students in a first practicum course. These student counselors conduct intake interviews and provide general counseling service to adolescent and adult clients at the Purdue Counseling and Guidance Center. All clients are self-referred, then evaluated for appropriateness via an intake interview. Some cases can be characterized as routine, whereas others may be quite challenging.

Doctoral student supervisors serve in the capacity of mentor and instructor. Although instructors of the counseling practicum retain full, absolute responsibility for formal evaluation and grading, the fact is that doctoral student supervisors are endowed with a significant amount of de facto evaluative influence. A great many issues arise from this factor, which exerts a major influence on the total experience.

Didactic Component

The didactic component is conducted using two texts: *Handbook of Counseling Supervision* (Borders & Leddick, 1987) and *Fundamentals of Clinical Supervision* (Bernard & Goodyear, 1992). Students also become familiar with the "Standards for Counseling Supervisors" (American Association for Counseling and Development, 1990) and the "Curriculum Guide for Training Counseling Supervisors" (Borders et al., 1991). Recommended reading includes *Psychotherapy Supervision: Theory, Research and Practice* (Hess, 1980) and *Supervising Counselors and Therapists: A Developmental Approach* (Stoltenberg & Delworth, 1987). Portions of the weekly class session are devoted to discussion of this material whenever possible within the context of current supervision activity.

Supervision Component

The supervision/consultation component consists of a weekly class session (or supervision conference) in which each of the student supervisors reports briefly on the week's activity. A topic or method is addressed each week either by instructor lecture or demonstration, or by class discussion. In a typical semester, there are 4–5 students in the supervision practicum, each of whom supervises three student counselors. During an ordinary week, there will have been at least 12–15 counselor-supervisor conferences to discuss progress with as many as 45 clients. The focus during these weekly class sessions is on supervision issues and methods, rather than the performance of the student counselors and progress (or lack of) being made by their clients. This volume of activity generates far more relevant conversation than there is usually time to complete. Therefore, it has been the practice to select weekly themes, following a developmental sequence, using current case work to illustrate supervision issues and interventions. Impromptu consultations during the week between the supervision practicum instructor and student supervisors are frequent. In addition, individual supervision sessions with student supervisors are conducted on a regular basis.

Summary of Activities

Students in the supervision practicum are instructed to do the following:

1. Attend and participate actively in a weekly 2 1/2-hour class session.
2. Complete readings as assigned.
3. Supervise three students in a beginning counseling practicum. Observe all intake interviews and as many other sessions as possible. Conduct a weekly supervision session with each counselor, in addition to brief, spontaneous consultations.
4. Meet individually with the supervision practicum instructor at least once every 3 weeks, in addition to frequent, spontaneous consultations.
5. Meet with instructors of the beginning practicum courses periodically at their request.
6. Conduct formal written and oral evaluations of each student at midterm and at semester end. The oral evaluation is conducted jointly with the student's practicum instructor.
7. Review, edit, revise, and approve all students' (those whom you supervise) intake, summary, and final reports, subject to review by the students' practicum instructor.

Evaluation and Grading

Feedback and evaluative comments are collected from all who have direct knowledge of the student supervisors' performance during the semester. For example, they are evaluated by each counselor whom they supervise at midterm and semester end. In addition, each practicum instructor evaluates every student supervisor with whom he or she has worked during the semester. A course grade is then assigned by the supervision practicum instructor using the following criteria:

- 40% Effectiveness as teacher/consultant
- 30% Executive skills (editing reports, monitoring student counselor's compliance with practicum instructor's directions, etc.)
- 15% Professional behavior (keeping appointments, observing sessions frequently)
- 15% Participation in class sessions

Summary of Strengths and Limitations

Strengths of the System

The system provides the student supervisor with a full, challenging, supervised experience in a clinic setting that serves as a laboratory in counseling and counselor supervision.

Student supervisors have constant access to consultation from two professionals: the supervision practicum instructor and the counseling practicum instructor. The system makes maximum use of the student supervisor's prior experience as counselor, teacher, or supervisor. The system allows the supervision practicum instructor and student supervisors to focus on supervision issues based on current experience without having to be also concerned with case-management issues, which are the domain of the counseling practicum instructor. The system significantly reduces the amount of direct observation and supervision that would otherwise be required of the counseling practicum instructor. Thus, the system facilitates the most efficient use of instructional resources.

Students in the beginning counseling practicum are provided a first-line supervisor who is more nearly a peer and with whom the issue of evaluation and grading is less immediate. Student supervisors participate in the evaluation process but do not bear responsibility for assigning grades in the counseling practicum. Performance evaluation is a complex task; students report that being able to observe faculty in this process is a valuable experience.

The system creates a series of teams, each containing a student counselor, a student supervisor, and a course instructor. Counselors have access to two levels of supervision while student supervisors learn to work cooperatively with three different teams, each with its own idiosyncrasies. Counseling practicum instructors are able to focus on developmental factors without feeling solely responsible for monitoring the status of all clients being seen by counselors in their practicum course.

Student supervisors have the advantage of two expert perspectives on each client: the practicum instructor and the supervision practicum instructor.

With few exceptions, students report that the supervision practicum is one of the most powerful learning events of their doctoral career, particularly with respect to (a) developing an instructional style, (b) learning to match the pace of learning according to a student's readiness and ability, (c) discovering the difference between authoritarian and authoritative, (d) seeing the effects of various counseling interventions in the lives of their student counselors' clients, (e) achieving greater resolution of their own power and control issues, and the like.

Student supervisors' performance is under the constant observation of both the supervision practicum instructor and the counseling practicum instructor. The system addresses all 11 "Standards for Counseling Supervisors" (American Association for Counseling and Development, 1990). All core content areas of the "Curriculum Guide for Supervisor Training" (Borders et al., 1991) are addressed in some way.

Limitations of the System

Student supervisors may not always be fully effective as counselors and/or educators, thus limiting the experience of students in the beginning counseling practicum. The system places significant responsibilities on student supervisors, some of whom may not be fully prepared for the multiple demands that are inherent in the role.

Large amounts of time and energy are required; doctoral students occasionally have other priorities and obligations (e.g., classes, mates, jobs, etc.) that complicate their lives. There is potential for confusion and competition between the counseling practicum instructor and the supervision practicum instructor. Students in the supervision practicum have sometimes (but only rarely) been caught between the opinions and preferences of these two authorities. This system is highly interdependent and thus requires very high levels of cooperation, communication, and commitment to professional excellence.

Implications and Questions

1. Having an on-campus counseling clinic provides an ideal setting in which to conduct a system for training doctoral-level supervisors.

2. Qualified doctoral student supervisors working under the supervision of counseling practicum instructors and the instructor of a supervision practicum enable significantly higher student-to-instructor ratios and, in addition, enable practicum instructors to attend more fully to teaching than to routine administrative and client-monitoring activities.

3. The equivalent of one full-time faculty member is required to administer an on-campus clinic: to provide prepracticum training and ongoing training and supervision for doctoral student supervisors.

4. What minimum levels of knowledge and skills preparation should be included in the doctoral program of counseling supervisors? Should there be a separate course for each component (didactic, skills laboratory, practicum)? What format is best? The system described here places greatest emphasis on practice and, except for a brief laboratory prior to the practicum, attempts to address all requisite knowledge and skills in a single course.

5. How is self-awareness of the student supervisor to be demonstrated and assessed? How are deficiencies to be corrected? This system acknowledges the importance of the question, but does not articulate how it might best be answered.

6. What portion of a counselor education program's total resources should be allocated to the preparation of supervisors? This question is compounded by the fact that supervisors in training provide valuable service at the same time. Another question should be asked simultaneously: Can an on-campus practicum be conducted in a cost-effective way without reliance on doctoral students or others who are similarly qualified?

7. What measures can be taken to prevent the exploitation of student supervisors in order to lighten faculty loads? This question should be addressed with care, but addressed nonetheless. It is not sufficient to rely exclusively on everyone's good nature, as may appear to be the case in the system described here.

References

American Association for Counseling and Development. (1990). Standards for counseling supervisors. *Journal of Counseling and Development, 69,* 30–32.

Borders, L. D., Bernard, J. M., Dye, H. A., Fong, M. L., Henderson, P., & Nance, D. W. (1991). Curriculum guide for training counseling supervisors: Rationale, development, and implementation. *Counselor Education and Supervision, 31,* 58–80.

Borders, L. D., & Leddick, G. R. (1987). *Handbook of counseling supervision.* Alexandria, VA: Association for Counselor Education and Supervision.

Bernard, J.M. (1979). Supervisor training: A discrimination model. *Counselor Education and Supervision, 19,* 740–748.

Bernard, J. M., & Goodyear, R. K. (1992). *Fundamentals of clinical supervision.* Boston: Allyn & Bacon.

Hess, A. K. (Ed.). (1980). *Psychotherapy supervision: Theory, research and practice.* New York: Wiley.

Kagan, N. (1980). Influencing human interaction—eighteen years with IPR. In A. K. Hess (Ed.), *Psychotherapy supervision: Theory, research and practice* (pp. 262–286). New York: Wiley.

Stoltenberg, C. D., & Delworth, U. (1987). *Supervising counselors and therapists: A developmental approach.* San Francisco: Jossey-Bass.

CHAPTER 16

PREPARATION OF DOCTORAL-LEVEL SUPERVISORS

John D. West
Donald L. Bubenzer
David L. Delmonico

At Kent State University in Kent, Ohio, the preparation of doctoral-level supervisors occurs through the Counseling and Human Development Center (CHDC). The CHDC is an in-house clinical-training center used by the Counseling and Human Development Services Program. This program involves doctoral-level preparation in Counselor Education and Supervision accredited by the Council for Accreditation of Counseling and Related Educational Programs (CACREP). During the academic year, the CHDC averages 500 client-contact hours per month, and about 80 students enroll in master's and doctoral-level practica per semester. A diagram of the CHDC is presented in Fig. 16.1. All but one of the rooms are equipped with one-way mirrors, videotape equipment, and intercom phones for phone-in supervision. The supervision of master's practicum students in the CHDC is part of the preparation for doctoral-level students in the counseling program. This doctoral-level preparation occurs through a three-credit course entitled "Supervision of Counseling." In this chapter, the authors describe the intentions, structure, and evaluation procedures of the course.

Intentions of the Course

Looking back at how "Supervision of Counseling" has been taught over the past 3 years, and considering its future, the following describe the intentions of the course:

1. Student supervisors are exposed to the three-tier supervision system in which they will work (i.e., their relationships with the instructor and supervisee, and the relationship between the supervisee and client). Liddle, Breunlin, Schwartz, and Constantine (1984) discussed this type of systemic relationship in training family-therapy supervisors. It appears that this model also has relevance when supervisees are learning individual therapy. Comments by Bernard and Goodyear (1992) indicated that supervisors are responsible for monitoring the quality of care provided to clients. Consequently, the two senior authors teach student supervisors to view this three-tier supervisory relationship as hierarchical in nature. Because the supervisor is ultimately responsible for the care provided to clients, one learns that one holds the top position in this hierarchy.

2. Student supervisors are assisted in appreciating the isomorphic nature of training and therapy. Liddle et al. (1984) discussed this issue in training family-therapy supervisors, but this dynamic also seems present when training supervisors for individual therapy supervision. For example, Liddle et al. suggested that the principle of "isomorphism" would indicate that the supervisor and supervisee are each interested in establishing a relationship, establishing goals, and challenging views of reality.

3. Student supervisors learn to help supervisees perceive/conceptualize cases from a theoretical model. The importance of these skills for supervisees has been suggested by Tomm and Wright (1979). They have discussed perceptual/conceptual skills for family therapists and refer to them as the ability to observe and make meaning out of client behavior. Perceptual/conceptual skills are also important for supervisees learning to do individual therapy, and the authors encourage student supervisors to be familiar with techniques designed to facilitate perceptual/conceptual skill development (e.g., audio- and videotape and case presentations). Moreover, Liddle et al. suggested the notion of expanding a supervisor's perceptual and conceptual focus from the family system to the therapeutic system, which includes the therapist plus the family. Student supervisors enrolled in the "Supervision of Counseling" course are also encouraged to develop skills in perceiving/conceptualizing the supervisee–client and supervisor–supervisee–client relationships, and similar objectives have also been suggested for those learning marital- and family-therapy supervision (Heath, 1989). (The American Associa-

tion for Marriage and Family Therapy Supervision Committee, 1991, has required members to meet objectives like these, in addition to other objectives, in order to supervise marital and family therapy.)

4. Student supervisors learn to help supervisees develop and use executive skills that influence the therapeutic relationship. The importance of these executive skills in family therapy has been discussed by Tomm and Wright (1979). They suggested that these skills are demonstrated through one's ability to channel emotional reactions to the client into therapeutic interventions. It appears that executive skills are not limited to family therapy, but are also important to the supervisee learning individual therapy. For example, these skills might include: (a) opening a session, (b) using reflection of feeling or summarization, (c) confronting discrepancies or teaching new cognitive skills, and (d) assigning homework. Moreover, student supervisors are encouraged to develop executive skills in structuring the supervision session and in implementing supervision interventions. Similar objectives have been suggested for those learning marital- and family-therapy supervision (Heath, 1989). (The American Association for Marriage and Family Therapy Supervision Committee, 1991, has required members to meet objectives similar to these, in addition to other objectives, in order to supervise marital and family therapy.)

5. Student supervisors start to view themselves as moving from being a direct service provider into the role of supervisor. For example, Hess (1986) suggested the early development of a student supervisor may be marked by focusing on the client and techniques that stimulate client change; as the student supervisor develops, he or she focuses more on the needs of the supervisee. The student supervisor also begins to consider legal and ethical issues involved in supervision. This professional transition into the role of a supervisor only begins to occur in a one-semester course.

Structure of the Course

As previously indicated, doctoral students in the Counseling and Human Development Services Program at Kent State University enroll in a one-semester course entitled "Supervision of Counseling." This class meets for 2½ hours each week. During the first hour of the class, the instructor provides a demonstration of supervision. The second half of the meeting is dedicated to discussion of supervision topics, such as the instructor's demonstration, supervision provided by students, assigned readings, or other ethicolegal issues.

First Hour of Class

During the first hour of the class, the instructor demonstrates supervision to a group of student supervisors by supervising a master's practicum student. During this time, the student supervisors observe the supervision in a fishbowl setting. For instance, the instructor might demonstrate assessing the supervisee's skill level with the Evaluation of Counselor Behaviors–Long Form (Bernard & Goodyear, 1992), or he or she might demonstrate the importance of being updated on all the supervisee's cases before focusing on skill development. The importance of staying current with all the supervisee's cases is congruent with the notion that supervisors are ultimately responsible for all of the supervisee's clients (Heath, 1990). This idea of legal and ethical responsibility is one that is emphasized throughout the course. The instructor might also demonstrate helping the supervisee perceive/conceptualize a case by using a format similar to the one presented by Loganbill and Stoltenberg (1983), or by using preselected segments of audio- or videotapes as suggested by Bernard and Goodyear (1992; e.g., segments showing the productive parts of a session, segments where the supervisee is struggling, or segments that depict recurring themes in therapy). The instructor might also use live supervision to demonstrate helping the supervisee develop executive skills and, thus, may use phone-ins as well as consultation breaks as methods of instruction.

The instructor concludes the demonstration by briefly talking with the student supervisors about the instructor–supervisee session. For example, they might discuss the instructor's use of supervision procedures (e.g., live or videotape procedures), the decision to use role-play in supervision, the procedures used to facilitate supervisee independence, as well as ethicolegal issues in supervision. These discussions focus on supervision issues that include facilitating the supervisee's perceptual/conceptual and executive skill development. The instructor also keeps boundaries clear between the student supervisors and the supervisee by having the student supervisors address their comments to the instructor rather than directly to the supervisee. During this question-and-comment time, the supervisee is allowed to simply listen in a manner similar to that of Anderson's (1991) reflecting teams. After the interchange between the instructor and the student supervisors is completed, the instructor asks the supervisee if he or she has any thoughts or questions concerning the supervision or comments made by class members. A short break is then taken before starting the second half of class.

Second Half of Class

In the second half of the class, any number of supervision issues can be discussed, and they often come from the student supervisors' experiences in providing supervision. Each student supervisor is assigned one master's practicum student to work with at the beginning of the semester. These supervisees come from practicum sections supervised by a different faculty member who is actually responsible for client care. The practicum instructor meets with the student supervisors weekly to monitor supervision and client progress. Discussions of supervision issues in the second half of the "Supervision of Counseling" class often focus on topics such as the isomorphic relationship between supervision and therapy. The following is an example of how the second half of class may proceed:

> For instance, after reviewing a videotaped supervision session, it was noted that the student supervisor spent much of the time teaching a supervisee to be more empathic. The student supervisor had previously also shared his observation that the supervisee was spending a lot of time in teaching related activities with clients. This student supervisor had been feeling unsuccessful at helping the supervisee use a broader array of therapeutic interventions (e.g., empathy). Consequently, it was suggested that the student supervisor increase his empathic statements concerning the supervisee's successes and frustrations in the practicum.

Discussions in the second half of the class have also concentrated on helping student supervisors focus more on supervisee behaviors, rather than client behaviors, while watching a videotape. To stimulate movement in this direction, the instructor on occasion might ask class members, "How can John focus more on the supervisee's development?" Discussions in the second half of the class have also considered the supervisee's ability to conceptualize cases and have considered the advantages of teaching the supervisee conceptual skills versus stimulating conceptual development via questioning, for example, "How would your theoretical model describe the client's presenting problem?" Procedures for facilitating the supervisee's executive skill development have also been discussed (e.g., live supervision, phone-ins, consultation breaks, and role-plays). For instance, the student supervisor could be asked to become the supervisee while another member of the class or the instructor takes the supervisor role. The role-play might focus on (a) reinforcing a supervisee for successful behaviors, (b) confronting a supervisee around nonproductive behaviors, or (c) teaching a supervisee new behaviors. The demonstration in the first half of the class and the discussion in the second half of the class are designed to help make the study of supervision applicable for the student supervisors. The two texts used most recently in "Supervision of Counseling" are *Fundamentals of Clinical Supervision* (Bernard & Goodyear, 1992) and *Supervising Counselors and Therapists* (Stoltenberg & Delworth, 1988).

Evaluation Procedures

Student supervisors are evaluated on the basis of three written assignments and their involvement in providing supervision to the master's practicum student. The first assignment has student supervisors describe any three models of supervision. The second assignment requires them to articulate their own personal model of supervision. Liddle et al. (1984) appeared to support the notion of articulating one's theoretical assumptions in training marital and family therapists, whereas Heath (1989) seemed to suggest procedures similar to the authors' for facilitating an understanding of supervision in marital and family therapy. (The American Association for Marriage and Family Therapy Supervision Committee, 1991, has required members to be able to describe several models as well as articulate a personal model of supervision, in addition to meeting other requirements, in order to supervise marital and family therapy.) In each of the papers for "Supervision of Counseling," student supervisors discuss (a) the goals of supervision models, (b) the nature of the supervisory relationship, (c) the procedures used by particular models of supervision, and (d) the methods used in evaluating supervisees.

Regarding the student supervisor's involvement in providing supervision to master's practicum students, the instructor evaluates the student supervisor by reviewing the supervisee's assessment of the supervision he or she received (see Bernard & Goodyear, 1992, for references on evaluating supervisors). The instructor also reviews the third of the three papers written by the student supervisor. This third paper is a case study in which the student supervisor describes his or her supervisee's level of skill development (perceptual/conceptual, executive), procedures employed in the supervision process, suggestions for future supervision of this supervisee, and an assessment of his or her own development as a supervisor. Student supervisors are encouraged to refer to *The Association for Counselor Education and Supervision Standards for Counselor Supervision* (Association for Counselor Education and Supervision Interest Network, 1989) as a resource in their self-evaluations.

Summary

The authors believe that the experiences in "Supervision of Counseling" can facilitate the student supervisor's movement toward seeing him or herself in a supervisory role. Important course experiences include: (a) observing and discussing demonstrations of a supervisory relationship, (b) providing supervision to a master's student, and (c) writing assignments that focus on comparing three models of supervision, developing one's own model, and the case study. Finally, the authors view this course as in the process of being developed. As a result, the authors encourage the reader to borrow that which seems useful and to modify that which seems inappropriate in one's own preparation of doctoral-level supervisors.

Implications

The following implications come from comments made in this chapter or from the authors' studies and experiences in supervision:

1. Preparation for becoming a supervisor is in addition to and differs from other types of direct services a counselor might provide (e.g., individual, group, or marital/family therapy).
2. Preparation for becoming a supervisor entails formal study as well as an opportunity to receive supervision of one's supervision style and skills. (See references cited in this chapter for a further discussion of issues related to becoming a supervisor.)
3. Preparation for becoming a supervisor is a developmental process that is not finished with the completion of an introductory course.

It is the authors' belief that an in-house training clinic such as the CHDC can facilitate efforts in supervising practicum students and in preparing students to become supervisors. Undoubtedly, there is room for additional thought regarding the preparation and supervision of supervisors, and the authors have appreciated the opportunity to share a part of their experience via the "think tank" on counselor education training laboratories at the 1992 ACES National Conference.

References

American Association for Marriage and Family Therapy Supervision Committee. (1991). *The A.A.M.F.T. approved supervisor designation: Standards and responsibilities.* Washington, DC: Author.

Anderson, T. (Ed.). (1991). *The reflecting team: Dialogues and dialogues about the dialogues.* New York: W.W. Norton.

Association for Counselor Education and Supervision Interest Network. (1989). *The Association for Counselor Education and Supervision Standards for Counselor Supervision.* Alexandria, VA: American Counseling Association.

Bernard, J. M., & Goodyear, R. K. (1992). *Fundamentals of clinical supervision.* Boston: Allyn & Bacon.

Heath, A. W. (Ed.). (1989). Learning objectives for supervision course. *A.A.M.F.T.: The Commission on Supervision Bulletin, II,* 2.

Heath, A. W. (Ed.). (1990). Legal liability in supervision: An interview with Steven L. Engelberg A.A.M.F.T. legal counsel. *A.A.M.F.T.: The Commission on Supervision Bulletin, III,* 2–4.

Hess, A. K. (1986). Growth in supervision: Stages of supervisee and supervisor development. *The Clinical Supervisor, 4,* 51–67.

Liddle, H. A., Breunlin, D. C., Schwartz, R. C., & Constantine, J. A. (1984). Training family therapy supervisors: Issues of content, form and context. *Journal of Marital and Family Therapy, 10,* 139–150.

Loganbill, C., & Stoltenberg, C. (1983). The case conceptualization format: A training device for practicum. *Counselor Education and Supervision, 22,* 235–241.

Stoltenberg, C.D., & Delworth, U. (1988). *Supervising counselors and therapists.* San Francisco: Jossey-Bass.

Tomm, K. M., & Wright, L. M. (1979). Training in family therapy: Perceptual, conceptual and executive skills. *Family Process, 18,* 227–250.

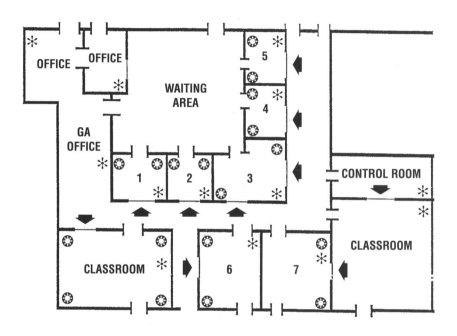

⊛ = Video Camera   ▶ = One Way Mirror   ✳ = Intercom Phone

Rooms 1 & 2 = 8ft x 8ft   Rooms 4 & 5 = 8ft x 8ft
Room 3 = 9ft x 12ft   Rooms 6 & 7 = 12ft x 17ft

**Figure 16.1
CHDC Floor Plan**

CHAPTER 17

REACTION: ON-CAMPUS TRAINING OF DOCTORAL-LEVEL SUPERVISORS

Janine M. Bernard

The models presented by Dye, and West and his colleagues, describing the training of doctoral supervisors at Purdue University and Kent State University, respectively, amply demonstrate the potential of counseling clinics to provide exemplary supervisor training. In addition to the breadth of issues addressed in these models, as well as the concentrated attention afforded each issue, one must appreciate the paradigm shift that these models illustrate from the training of supervisors a generation ago. The need for supervisor training has been argued adequately elsewhere (Bernard, 1981; Borders & Leddick, 1987). However, by virtue of this training a new collaborative vision of supervision has emerged. In other words, where supervision has been an isolating experience in the past, training models, including those described by Dye and West, introduce professional collaboration right from the outset. This has the potential of influencing the profession of counseling as much as any knowledge or skill acquisition embedded in the training.

Complexity of Supervisor-Training Models

As I reviewed the two models presented in this book, I found myself appreciating anew the complexity of developing a supervisor-training model within a clinic setting. It seems that the complexity is experienced conceptually, administratively, and systemically by those involved.

The conceptual challenge of training doctoral supervisors begins, as Borders (1989) pointed out, with helping the supervisor in training begin to think like a supervisor. Adding another level to the therapeutic system can be a difficult (if not mind-boggling) conceptual stretch for many doctoral students. Even if this shift is relatively painless, the practice of supervision can appear to include the entire knowledge base of the profession: theoretical approaches to counseling, models of supervision, cultural dimensions of interactions at both the counseling and supervisory level, ethical and legal imperatives, executive skills, and so on. While juggling conceptually, those involved in a training clinic become aware of the administrative complexities that are part of daily operations. There are practicum students who have some relationship to students in a supervision practicum. Each of these practica have a faculty instructor and, of course, there is usually a director of the counseling clinic who must be kept abreast of issues that arise. Records must be kept of counseling, supervision, and supervision of supervision. Referrals are made, intakes are done, summary reports are written, and evaluations are completed. What looks like the straightforward delivery of counseling to clients is supported by a highly complicated series of procedures and relationships.

The administrative complexity is related to the systemic complexity of the clinic that attempts to train supervisors. Roles are varied and complex. Dye referred to the possibility that there may be confusion or competition between the instructors of the practicum and the supervision practicum. Even in the best of clinic "families," communication can break down when folks get busy. But when power is an issue, coalitions can develop that will certainly compromise the training received by doctoral supervisors who are often parentified children in the system.

Dual Agendas

Another reality for counseling clinics that also serve as training clinics is the challenge of meeting related but different sets of agendas. Part of the intricacy of the training models presented by Dye and West et al. was an attempt to meet both educational and clinical demands adequately. Although there are many examples of competing agendas within a training clinic setting, I limit my discussion to two issues because of space constraints.

The first issue is the most obvious. Unlike other counseling centers, the training clinic is attempting to serve two masters. Some clinics attempt to reduce their dilemma by declaring their loyalty: "We are first and foremost in the business of providing counseling to clients," or "We are first and foremost a training clinic for counselors and supervisors."

(Of course such a declaration is an illusion of safety if the legal world should ever come crashing in.) Usually clinic personnel want to provide sound counseling *and* sound training. Only the best of clinics (including the two presented in this book) can begin to accomplish such an ambitious task. Yet, even the best of clinics can lose sight of one of their missions when clients need to be served, practicum students need to be supervised, and doctoral students need to be provided the opportunity to supervise. The orchestration of these different constituencies and the meeting of their various needs in a way that is professional, ethical, and efficient calls for well-honed executive skills (Bernard & Goodyear, 1992).

Another common dilemma within a training clinic is the tension between the educational agenda for the training of supervisors and the real supervision issues that occur during a supervision practicum. The solution, of course, is to require didactic and prepracticum experiences in supervision prior to assigning supervisees to the doctoral supervisor. Although the models presented by Dye and West et al. address the issue of prerequisites, many doctoral programs attempt to "do it all" in one curricular experience. The result is that reflective integration of the supervision literature is far more difficult to accomplish.

Observations and Implications

Both Dye and West et al. presented doctoral supervisor-training sequences that represent "state-of-the art" models. The following observations outline additional issues to those highlighted by these authors:

1. Much has been said about the advantages of the on-campus training clinic. The control that the faculty enjoy over the training experience is enviable. At the same time, can the amount of control become too much of a good thing? Does a training clinic simulate other clinical settings? Will doctoral supervisors be adequately prepared to supervise off-campus when the organizational culture may not be as conducive to supervisory goals? Should doctoral students be required to supervise off-campus as well as within an on-campus clinic?

2. When on-campus clinics are absent, practicum students are assigned to off-campus settings that are related to their career goals. In these cases, counselors receive supervision from experienced practitioners on-site, practitioners who share the career goals of the student. Doctoral students usually have career goals that are quite different from their

practicum student supervisees. Is anything lost when master's practicum students are supervised by doctoral students who have different career aspirations (Bernard, 1992)?

3. Finally, it is important to put the training of doctoral supervisors in context. In a survey of Council for Accreditation of Counseling and Related Educational Programs (CACREP) master's programs (Bernard, 1992), the great majority of on-site supervisors (over 70%) of practicum and internship students held the master's as their terminal degree. Therefore, the assumption of virtually all training clinics that supervision is a doctoral-level activity was not supported by this survey. Most supervision occurring in the field is conducted by experienced practitioners who hold a master's degree and use an apprenticeship model to conduct supervision. Consequently, doctoral-level clinical-training directors seem to be in danger of creating supervisors in their own images, whereas supervision in the field remains virtually untouched and unchallenged.

References

Bernard, J. M. (1981). Inservice training for clinical supervisors. *Professional Psychology, 12,* 740–748.

Bernard, J. M. (1992). Training master's level counseling students in the fundamentals of clinical supervision. *The Clinical Supervisor, 10,* 133–143.

Bernard, J. M., & Goodyear, R. K. (1992). *Fundamentals of clinical supervision.* Needham Heights, MA: Allyn & Bacon.

Borders, L. D. (1989, August). *Learning to think like a supervisor.* Paper presented at the annual meeting of the American Psychological Association, New Orleans, LA.

Borders, L. D., & Leddick, G. R. (1987). *Handbook of counseling supervision.* Alexandria, VA: Association for Counselor Education and Supervision.

PART VI

COUNSELOR EDUCATION LABORATORIES AS MENTAL HEALTH CLINICS

CHAPTER 18

COUNSELOR EDUCATION CLINICS AS COMMUNITY RESOURCES

George R. Leddick

The clinic with which this author is familiar is housed in a state university enrolling 12,000 students in a city of about 350,000 people. It is not affiliated with the dean of students' services and has a separate campus location. The clinic is composed of seven counseling/observation rooms with one-way mirrored glass, a seminar room, and reception and file areas. Operating 4 evenings per week, the clinic typically serves 70 individual clients and 24 group clients each semester. Portions of most sessions are observed by faculty supervisors. The median number of sessions per client, including dropouts, is eight. Clients range in age from 5 to 68 years old; 70% are children between 11–15 years of age. Clients are referred by counselors in 26 public schools in five nearby school systems, by campus counseling services, campus services for students with disabilities, a campus center for women and returning adults, and three state rehabilitation services. Typical client issues include: (a) remarriage and stepfamily issues, (b) depression, (c) career counseling, (d) life transitions, (e) eating disorders, (f) parenting and child discipline, (g) coping with loss, (h) self-concept enhancement, and (i) relationship issues.

This chapter focuses primarily on the counselor education clinic's visibility in the community. The clinic's perceived community presence is determined through three factors: (a) marketing image, (b) client expectations, and (c) access. Each is described in turn.

Marketing

There are three ways that counselor education clinics are viewed as community resources. When large universities inhabit small towns, the clinic might serve as one of only two available service agencies. When this is the case, the clinic is driven, in large measure, to meet local needs for services. Another model for marketing a clinic is as a competitive business. If the university is accustomed to generating revenue from the clinic, a dean might insist that the clinic generate a specific level of fees or face a reduction in personnel. One example of this model is when a university implementing "responsibility center" management influenced a clinic to implement 30-minute counseling sessions to generate additional income. There was no relationship of session length to a new emphasis on brief or solution-focused therapy. In this model, revenue production supersedes training practices. The clinic is a business first and training center second.

The third model of clinic marketing is the provision of services to underserved populations. Here, training drives service provision and the university benefits primarily from positive public relations as a community benefactor. The clinic does not compete aggressively for the same clients served by other agencies.

Respective priorities of service, economy, or training are not mutually exclusive. They are norms found in every counselor education clinic and are dealt with either consciously or unconsciously. Once these priorities are decided consciously, publicizing the clinic's mission will be more precisely and clearly stated.

Should Clinics Charge Fees?

The decision to charge fees for services is directly related to clinic priorities of service versus economy versus training. The research on this topic is sparse and typically consists of surveys of university counseling centers, not counselor education clinics.

There are two questions addressed in the literature: (a) Do we charge fees? and (b) Should we? Four studies address the former question. Nugent and Pareis (1968) found that 4% of 141 university counseling centers charged fees. Hurst, Davidshofer, and Arp (1974) also cited only 4% charging fees. More recently (Hughes & Benson, 1986), researchers reported that 56 of 72 counseling centers charged fees. In that study, 42 counseling centers employed a sliding scale to determine fees, and 14 charged the same nominal fee to all clients. To the contrary, a more current survey (Stone & Archer, 1990) found that three fourths of the responding counseling centers did not charge fees. However, one third of those providing free services anticipated charging user fees in the future.

Should clinics charge fees? Yokun and Berman (1984) cited a 1913 statement by Freud suggesting that payment of fees may contribute to the success of treatment. Those authors agreed with Freud, finding that fee-paying clients expected to gain more from treatment than did non-paying clients. Conoley and Bonner (1991) reported that fees were positively correlated with perceptions of counselor credibility, attractiveness, and expertness. The higher the fee level, the greater credibility accorded to the counselor. However, Subich and Hardin (1985) found the existence of fees did not affect the motivation for, evaluation of, or willingness to seek counseling. Those authors also cited counseling-center directors' concerns. Would charging a fee discourage use of the counseling center? Would fees encourage remediation practices and discourage preventative and developmental programming? Is it unfair to university students, especially at expensive private schools, to levy additional charges when they are already paying tuition and fees? Further research is necessary to determine how fees might affect client motivation.

Managing Client Expectations

Results of a survey by Whiteley, Mahaffey, and Leer (1987) identified five types of university counseling centers. Macrocenters offer a broad array of services including career and personal counseling, testing, training and consultation, and limited academic advising. Career Planning and Placement Centers feature career-oriented services with minimal supplementary services. Counseling Orientation Centers are similar to macrocenters, but offer fewer career services. General Level Service Centers include a wider variety of services in addition to counseling. Minimal Services Centers feature few services in all areas. Identifying the extent and type of services available helps clients identify whether your clinic is appropriate to their needs.

At the author's university, clients are typically referred by off-campus counselors and are not often self-referred. To help clarify client expectations, all clients receive two brochures and an intake form prior to their arrival on campus. One brochure lists "Client Rights and Responsibilities," and various versions of this brochure are available from Chi Sigma Iota or the National Board for Certified Counselors. Our version also includes statements delineating the limits of confidentiality, in the event clients may be of harm to selves or others, or commit child abuse. Our second brochure (a) describes examples of specific services available at our clinic, (b) identifies the existence of professional ethical standards and an address for consumer complaints, and (c) describes the training and professional credentials of six faculty supervisors. The latter is mandated by state law certifying counseling professionals.

These descriptive written materials augment a 20-minute telephone call for each client. Our telephone calls have been scripted by a telephone intake form available to all who staff intake. This brings more uniformity to the information both given and gathered by phone.

Access for Off-Campus Clients

Serving as a community resource means attracting a significant number of off-campus clients. Some clients may need directions to locate the campus and gain access to parking. Our client brochure includes a campus map, indicating the location of both the clinic and adjacent parking. Our counselor education clinic location is posted in the building's directory, and the clinic is listed separately in the campus telephone book. Each client also receives a business card for the counselor education clinic, giving a voice-mail telephone number in the event of an emergency or cancellation. Faculty monitor messages on the voice-mail system daily. On weekends and holidays, emergency calls can be automatically forwarded to faculty home phones. Campus telephone systems without voice-mail capabilities can be upgraded by addition of a $250 interface card for either Apple or IBM-compatible desktop computers.

Communication Outreach

In addition to frequent communications with off-campus clients, interagency and intraagency communication must be continuously fostered. Because our clinic relies primarily on counselor referrals, liaison with these professionals is important. We expedite this by incorporating a "permission to contact" form on our intake form. Clients thereby routinely grant us permission to contact their referring counselor, but only to tell them when they initiate and terminate counseling. Additional information requires separate client permission. Mail-merge letters on a word processor are routinely sent to follow-up on clients, and also to encourage school counselors to identify new clients early in the semester.

Because faculty have desktop computers, each has access to electronic mail charts for client scheduling. A disk-lock software program ensures limited access to confidential client information. Student counselors are provided a clinic operations manual describing: (a) typical center procedures, (b) client file forms and how to complete them, (c) emergency procedures, (d) child abuse reporting (how to instruct/protect the client), (e) policies for confronting sexual attraction to clients, (f) HIV-positive clients and "danger to others," and (g) ethical standards.

Summary

Counselor education clinics can provide a variety of services and are driven by several priorities: (a) service, (b) economy, or (c) training. Once your clinic's specific combination of characteristics is determined, these must be communicated to the community. Marketing your clinic is vital for establishing client expectations. Liaison with referral sources, student counselors, and faculty supervisors is continuous and can be automated through the use of desktop computers.

Implications

1. Research on the effects of clinic fees must identify categories of sliding scale versus nominal fees versus high fees and compare whether clinics have priorities of service, profit, or training.
2. Desktop publishing, electronic mail, and voice-mail are methods of automating continuous requirements for communication among various community constituencies.

References

Conoley, T. C., & Bonner, M. (1991). The effects of counselor fee and title on perceptions of counselor behavior. *Journal of Counseling and Development, 69,* 356–358.

Hughes, T. N., & Benson, A. J. (1986). University clinics as field placement and school psychology training: A national survey. (ERIC Document Reproduction Service No. ED 260 329) Greensboro, NC: ERIC/CASS.

Hurst, T. C., Davidshofer, C. O., & Arp, S. (1974). Current perceptions and practices of charging fees in college and university counseling centers. *Journal of Counseling Psychology, 21*(6), 532–535.

Nugent, F. A., & Pareis, E. N. (1968). Survey of present policies and practices in college counseling centers in the United States of America. *Journal of Counseling Psychology, 15*(1), 94–97.

Stone, G. L., & Archer, T. (1990). College and university counseling centers of the 1990's: Challenges and limits. *The Counseling Psychologist, 16*(1), 539–607.

Subich, L. M., & Hardin, S. I. (1985). Counseling expectations as a function of fee for service. *Journal of Counseling Psychology, 32*(3), 323–328.

Whiteley, S., Mahaffey, P. T., & Leer, C. A. (1987). The campus counseling center: A profile of staffing patterns and services. *Journal of College Student Personnel, 28*, 71–81.

Yokun, C., & Berman, J. S. (1984). Does paying fee for psychotherapy alter the effectiveness of treatment? *Journal of Consulting and Clinical Psychology, 52*(2), 254–260.

CHAPTER 19

A COOPERATIVE TRAINING CLINIC AS A MENTAL HEALTH CENTER

Michael K. Altekruse
Judith Seiters

Southern Illinois University at Carbondale (SIUC) has developed a unique concept to provide for the clinical-training needs of the university. Over 30 years ago, a cooperative clinical center was formed at SIUC with five functioning divisions: Psychological Services, Physical Therapy Services, Reading Services, Social Work Services, and Speech and Hearing Services. Since then, the Achieve Program was added to provide services for learning-disabled SIUC students. These divisions collaborate to share space and resources. The primary purposes of the Clinical Center, which is described in this chapter, are:

1. To assist academic departments in preparing students for professional careers in clinical fields by providing and maintaining a professional facility in which clinical practicum can be conducted under proper supervision.
2. To provide a clinical facility in which faculty who teach clinical skills cannot only supervise students in practicum but can also work with clients to maintain and further develop their own clinical expertise.
3. To make a variety of high-quality professional services available to university students and the general public.
4. To maintain facilities and programs that allow faculty and students from different clinical disciplines to stimulate and learn from one another through close interaction in a clinical setting.

5. To provide a climate that encourages and supports student and faculty research involving the identification or alleviation of clinical problems.

The SIUC Clinical Center

The Clinical Center is administered by a director who reports to the associate vice president for academic affairs. This reporting occurs because the Clinical Center's service divisions cross over a number of departmental and college lines. Service coordinators represent the professional divisions and (a) administer professional policy, (b) evaluate intake information, (c) assign cases, (d) assume responsibility for programming, and (e) maintain necessary administrative-professional relationships between the center, other professional persons, agencies, and the general public. A Clinical Center Council, consisting of the service coordinators and representatives from participating departments, acts as an advisory group to the director in establishing professional policies and making decisions regarding other aspects of the center's operation.

In any given year, 200–250 practicum students from nine academic units in five schools and colleges are involved in clinical training and research activities in the Clinical Center. The academic units utilizing the center for practicum training include the College of Communications and Fine Arts (Department of Communication Disorders and Sciences), the College of Education (Department of Curriculum and Instruction, Department of Educational Psychology, Department of Special Education, Department of Physical Education, and the Rehabilitation Institute), the College of Liberal Arts (Department of Psychology), the College of Technical Careers (Physical Therapist Assistant Program), and the School of Social Work. Typically, Clinical Center practicum students and professional staff provide direct service to over 2,000 individuals a year. Slightly less than half of these individuals are SIUC students; the remainder are children and adults from over 33 Illinois counties, as well as from several other states. These clients keep over 30,000 appointments each year, resulting in over 40,000 client-contact hours.

The Clinical Center receives funding for its operation from the vice president for academic affairs. In addition, all clients not connected with the university are assessed service fees. The director and support staff are full-time employees. Professional staff, including the service coordinators, have split appointments in their respective departments and the

Clinical Center, and are paid by each unit according to the percentage of their assignment.

Psychological Services Division

The Psychological Services Division of the center serves as the primary on-campus preinternship site for clinical training of graduate students in several academic programs. As a training unit, the Psychological Services Division provides comprehensive mental health services for SIUC and the local community. Services offered include: (a) psychological testing, (b) learning-disability testing, (c) neuropsychological testing, (d) biofeedback, (e) individual and group counseling, (f) marriage and family counseling, (g) rehabilitation counseling, and (h) psychiatric services.

Students within the Psychological Services Division are assigned to the center from the Department of Educational Psychology (Counselor Education and School Psychology), the Psychology Department (Clinical Psychology), the Rehabilitation Institute (Behavior Modification and Rehabilitation Counseling), and the Department of Special Education (Learning Disabilities). The Clinical Center also serves as a major campus research setting for clinically oriented research projects conducted by staff members, departmental faculty, and graduate students.

Clients are often referred to the Clinical Center from the SIUC Counseling Center (which employs a brief therapy model—12 appointment limit), the SIUC Health Services, local mental health units, and private practitioners. However, most clients are self-referrals. After making contact, clients are assigned a social work intake appointment and, if they are adults, a psychological intake. Marriage and family cases and adult clients receive a separate second intake for research purposes. After orientation and training, students conduct both the social work and the psychological intakes.

After prospective clients complete their intakes, the reports are given to the coordinator of Psychological Services, who assigns the clients to student or faculty clinicians and practicum teams. Faculty supervisors from the participating departments assume primary responsibility for the direction of the diagnostic and therapeutic work with the clients and provide close supervision of student clinical activity. The center's budgeted staff work primarily with clients whose problems require experience or skills beyond those yet acquired by graduate students. The center also employs a quarter-time psychiatrist who works with Clinical Center clients and serves as a psychiatric consultant for staff and graduate students.

Thus, the center is able to provide treatment for a full spectrum of behavioral and emotional problems. Budgeted staff members are also able to provide on-site consultation for graduate students working with clients in the center. In most cases, the budgeted staff members also serve as departmental clinical instructors/supervisors, so their clinical activities contribute to the development of their teaching skills.

Each year, approximately 100 graduate students work with clients in the Psychological Services Division of the center. Some of these students obtain primarily counseling or psychotherapeutic experience, some primarily psychodiagnostic experience, and some a combination of both. The students assigned to the center are supported by 3.50 full-time equivalent (FTE) budgeted and assigned Psychological Services staff, a .25 FTE psychiatrist, three .50 FTE graduate assistant clinicians, one .50 FTE graduate administrative assistant, and one .60 FTE coordinator. The intensity of student involvement with clients varies widely from student to student, with some students spending 20 hours a week in field placement or internship and some only 1 hour a week in beginning practicum. Those students involved in counseling each work with approximately three cases during the year, whereas those involved primarily in psychodiagnostic training work with approximately eight cases each. Budgeted staff members see approximately 10 clients per week and may also participate in assigned research. Staff not assigned to the clinic may request appointment as nonpaid clinical staff volunteers for research and client service.

Beyond direct services to clients, some of the Psychological Services Division staff members are involved in area service and clinical research. The research projects are psychological in nature and are usually conducted in the Clinical Center. The assigned service is also psychological in nature and gives the clinic positive exposure while providing important service to the area.

During 1991–1992, Clinical Center staff and supervised students saw over 460 counseling cases for 4,396 contact hours, and completed 92 psychological evaluations for 1.125 contact hours, 37 psychiatric evaluations for 21 contact hours, and 66 pharmocotherapy cases for 101 contact hours. Over 150 clients received group counseling for 1,447 contact hours. The breadth and depth of this activity is typical of the services provided by the Psychological Services Division during any given year.

The Department of Educational Psychology

Within the Department of Educational Psychology, there are three Council for Accreditation of Counseling and Related Educational Programs (CACREP) accredited programs (School Counseling, Community Counseling, and the PhD in Counselor Education), as well as a program in School Psychology. A program in Marriage and Family Counseling is a cooperative venture with Clinical Psychology. The department conducts all of its practica in the Clinical Center, with clients appropriate for each student's major area of emphasis. Students in Community Counseling often do their internships in the Clinical Center working with clients from the local and surrounding community. School Counseling students' internship sites are in the schools; however, these students often see age-appropriate clients in the Clinical Center. Because the center is open in the evenings, the students are afforded additional opportunities to complete their internship requirements.

The department is required to provide individual and group supervision according to the CACREP standards (1 hour a week individual and 1½ hours of group supervision) for all practica and internship students. Supervision is part of the faculty members' class assignment. Some faculty are assigned to the center as part of their faculty load at a percentage ranging from 33% to 67%. Faculty who are assigned to the Clinical Center provide direct service, but may also be assigned research time or the supervision of interns.

Due to the multidisciplinary nature of the Clinical Center, there are opportunities to work with students and faculty from various departments. For example, Clinical Psychology and Counselor Education are cooperating in the Marriage and Family program with faculty from both departments teaching and supervising practicum students in both programs. A research database has been established with all adult clients. This database is being used for research by students and faculty from all participating departments. In addition, students and faculty from different departments have served as cotherapists and often help each other in peer supervision.

Summary

The idea of a cooperative training center originated at SIUC over 30 years ago. Since that time, other institutions have investigated the plan and in many cases have established centers similar to the one described herein. A cooperative center offers many advantages to participating departments. Economically, it is less expensive than running an independent or decentralized training clinic because of the shared expense. Faculty stay current with their clinical skill development because at least a small percentage of their work assignment is as a clinician. Shared income provides opportunities to purchase "state-of-the-art" equipment and materials. In addition, faculty and students have the opportunity to work with and learn from faculty and students in other disciplines. The clinic has provided cooperative ventures with other departments, including a Marriage and Family program. This cooperation has resulted in shared research, presentations, and publications.

Disadvantages are also shared in such a venture. With so many disciplines sharing the same space, it is often difficult getting a room, especially between 4:00 p.m. and 9:00 p.m. It is also sometimes difficult to share the same space when you have different objectives as professionals, belong to different professional organizations, abide by different ethical codes, and have separate accreditation and licensure requirements. In such a situation, however, disciplines have to learn to live with their differences and to clearly define their roles as human service professionals. For example, counselor educators and clinical psychologists were forced to demonstrate and explain how they were similar and how they differed from each other. This produced some testy times, but produced a healthy result.

Implications for Training Centers

1. With financial cutbacks being forced on most higher education institutions, departments may be forced to examine the cooperative clinic model presented here. Cooperating with other departments to present an on-site clinic has benefits that exceed financial considerations. At SIUC, a cooperative relationship and understanding were developed between counselor education, rehabilitation, social work, and psychology. Differences are understood and valued.

2. With the present concern of proliferating professions, the cooperative clinic model may be one that aids in new understanding and respect between the helping professions. At SIUC, we not only worked with each other, but often we also presented and wrote together. Students benefited greatly from this cooperative relationship because

they learned to work with students and professors from other departments.

3. The cooperative clinic described here is a great research base for students and faculty. With the Clinical Center staff and supervised students seeing over 460 counseling cases, 92 psychological evaluations, 37 psychiatric evaluations, 66 pharmocotherapy cases, and over 150 clients in groups each year, it is easy to see the research possibilities for both students and faculty.

4. The chapters in this book provide the opportunity to explore problems with on-site clinics, but also give an opportunity to find solutions. We encourage the Association for Counselor Education and Supervision (ACES) to continue to give its membership the opportunity to solve some of the major problems facing the profession today. We recommend a similar format for future conventions and an ongoing ACES interest group on on-site clinics.

CHAPTER 20

DUAL ROLE OR CONFLICT OF INTEREST? CLINICS AS MENTAL HEALTH PROVIDERS

Jane E. Myers
Gerald H. Hutchinson

Various methods of utilizing a counselor education clinic facility have been discussed in this book, including use of the facility for supervised prepracticum, practicum, and internship training, research, and community mental health services. There are perhaps as many different ways of designing and utilizing clinics as there are counselor education programs and communities to serve. Several distinct models for operating counselor-training clinics have been presented in this book (see chapters 5, 16, 18, and 19). This chapter includes discussion of concerns germane to any clinic facility, which, although being used primarily as a training site, also seeks to service clients from the community. Although training may be the sole reason the clinic was established, when clients from the community are served the facility also becomes, to a greater or lesser extent, a community mental health agency. This dual role can be the source of excellent training for students while creating a dual role for the facility. As always occurs in dual role situations, conflicts of interest arise. The nature of some of these conflicts, as expressed in the chapters by Leddick (chapter 18) and Altekruse and Seiters (chapter 19), are reviewed herein.

Mission and Goals

Administrative and operational conflicts arise when a clinic seeks to operate as both a training facility and a mental health agency. The needs of two separate and distinct populations (i.e., counselors in training and clients) must be served, and these needs often conflict. On the one hand, students with perhaps little prior counseling experience need clients with whom they can take risks and make mistakes in order to learn and practice counseling skills and learn first hand what is meant by the counseling process. On the other hand, clients deserve to receive the best counseling services possible. Students often must learn from their mistakes, which may result in ineffective, awkward, or inappropriate services. The conflicting needs of these populations may be resolved through careful creation, planning, and implementation of the training-clinic mission.

Clearly articulated mission and goals statements endorsed by the teaching faculty, the clinic director, and the university administration are essential to the effective operation of the clinic. Mission and goals statements are drawn to articulate purpose and targeted activities. Common purposes include: (a) providing training facilities; (b) serving clients; (c) performing research; and (d) communicating practice, research, and theory issues to the professional community through workshops and seminars. The mission charts the intended purpose for the clinic's existence, and the goals operationalize the mission so that progress can be measured. The clinic with an uncertain mission or ill-defined goals will flounder with much wasted energy on the part of persons responsible for the direction and implementation of clinic activities.

The role of the counseling clinic must be resolved as integral to defining a mission and the subsequent goals that flow from that identity. Common roles include that of (a) training laboratory, (b) research facility, and (c) mental health agency. Some clinics operate solely as training labs for students, in which students alternately play roles of counselor, client(s), and supervisors (e.g., for prepracticum only). Other clinics operate in this manner, and also open their doors to members of the community so that "real persons with real problems" may receive counseling (e.g., the practicum experience). These arrangements mean that the counseling staff must be clearly identified; have minimal training adequate to the clients' presenting issues; and that the nature of their training, competence, and supervision be articulated to all clients.

Recruiting Clients

Recruiting the "right" kind of client for the clinic purpose is an important function. If the clinic provides service to the community and generates a "good" reputation, self-referral of clients is likely to result in some who are inappropriate for the students in training. Again, the mission and goals statements will assist the clinic staff in determining recruitment sources and in educating potential referral sources as to the nature of the clinic services and appropriate clientele.

If the clinic is operating solely as a training lab, student volunteers from graduate and undergraduate classes may be recruited. Of course, all efforts must be made to protect the confidentiality of clients. This can become an especially difficult concern when fellow graduate students (i.e., peers) are used as clients.

When the clinic operates as a mental health agency, recruitment sources for community members can be other counselors and counseling services, hospitals and physicians, and private psychiatric hospitals. Community colleges and university continuing education departments can be excellent sources for career-counseling clients. Because many universities and colleges operate on an academic calendar, where 12-month supervision may not be available, clients able to identify and work toward goals that are achievable in a short time period may be more appropriate for the clinic than those whose needs may best be met by long-term counseling.

One particularly sensitive issue becomes the recruitment of community clients, especially when nominal or no fees are assessed for services, as this may present competition with local private practitioners. This concern may be acute in smaller towns and cities where the potential client base is smaller. In larger cities, this concern may be mediated by the perception that students being trained in counseling have less expertise and credibility than private practitioners.

In our own clinic, we have found that the preparation and dissemination of a flyer describing our services to local practitioners and agencies has been a useful means of generating appropriate referrals. Such brochures need not be elaborate. Our own is only one page in length (see Appendix G). Intake counselors in other agencies have asked for multiple copies in order to provide them to prospective clients.

Screening for Appropriate Clientele

When clinic-counseling services are made available to community members, screening criteria are an essential means of determining both suitable and unsuitable clients. Decisions such as the hours of clinic operation may be guided by the type of presenting client concerns. Because acute or chronic client problems could require 24-hour availability of staff, a decision to limit client concerns to less acute and chronic problems may be prudent. Acute and chronic clients would be screened out and referred to the county mental health agency or other practitioners, whereas clients may be actively recruited who indicate concerns that can be addressed through weekly sessions for a period that does not exceed the length of the academic term.

Screening of clients for suitability of the clinic services (as determined by staff training and experience, and supervisory input) must be undertaken by a trained clinician. A standard intake procedure should be used that includes some form of mental status exam and psychosocial history. If multiple intake counselors are used, this process becomes paramount to ensure both standardization of procedures and the availability of adequate client information for optimal case management. Ideally, an advanced doctoral student, faculty member, or credentialled practitioner would perform the intake role. Supervised intake activities conducted by doctoral students can be an important training experience for later postdoctoral clinical work.

Establishing Conditions for the Receipt of Service

The intake/screening interview also should cover client consent for the receipt of services, which may be conditional to the clinic mission and goals. For instance, utilization of training procedures (i.e., videotaping of sessions and use of tapes for supervision purposes) may be a necessary condition. Client rights and responsibilities should be discussed and clients may be provided with a copy of the brochure "Client Rights and Responsibilities" (Chi Sigma Iota/National Board for Certified Counselors, 1989), which provides a brief, readable summary of important counseling consumer information. Any limitations or special conditions imposed by the academic calendar or by the training requirements of student counselors should be addressed. Fees charged and billing procedures need to be discussed. Taking factors from the intake assessment into consideration, assignment of the client to a counselor may be coordinated by the intake counselor or the clinic director.

Arranging a fee schedule suitable to the mission of the clinic also can become complex. Considerations include: (a) whether the university will allow the clinic to charge for services, (b) what counselors in the community charge, and (c) what other public counseling services charge. The lowest and highest fee and determination of the type of fees (e.g., flat fee, tiered-fee schedule, sliding-fee scale) should follow, again, from the limitations of the previous considerations and the clinic mission.

Should university students be clients, a conflict of interest may arise with the student counseling service, if one exists. University fees for students regularly include free access to counseling services as needed through the student counseling center. A counselor education training clinic charging students for services may be at odds with university policy. Such charges may arouse concern among parents, providing financial support for their children, who believe they already have paid usage fees should their children need assistance. The sentiment that publicly funded institutions should not charge for any services to the community may need to be addressed when a fee schedule is determined.

Counselor Supervision

Supervision becomes an acute concern when community members become clients. Liability falls on the college, the counselor education faculty, the clinic director, the supervisor, and the student should there be a claim. The possibility of litigation necessitates a thoughtful approach to the mission, administrative support, and logistics and quality of supervision. Discussions with the college or university attorney can be very helpful in determining liability coverage needs, as discussed in chapter 9. Administrative support for the clinic as a mental health agency must be overtly provided by the university. It is not sufficient and potentially dangerous to assume that a small scope of services alleviates the need for legal consultation. Our own university attorney was very clear on this issue: A first semester master's student engaging in a course-related practicum experience with a client who is enrolled in an undergraduate career and life-planning course, and is attending counseling as a client to gain course credit, is still subject to litigation. The master's student is seen as "an agent of the state" providing professional counseling services to an informed client. All counseling students, as well as all faculty members in the department, need to carry professional liability insurance to protect them in the event of a lawsuit.

Once clients have been matched with counselors and sessions have begun, supervision should be provided as a means of case management and counselor training. Supervision may occur through either case-load management or case sampling. Case-load management describes the thorough process of reviewing every client file on a regular basis (e.g., once a week, every other week). In addition to this method, case consultations may occur once a week or on an as-needed basis. Clinic staffings may be held periodically to review difficult cases and to get input from all clinical staff on the handling of the counseling process.

Case sampling describes the process whereby the clinical staff member presents a limited number of cases (perhaps only one) from his or her case-load, and the supervisor addresses these issues as if they represent either the bulk of client issues, or the difficult case(s). The drawback to case load management is that, although thorough, it is quite time-consuming. The drawback to case sampling is that, although convenient, it may not be adequate for all cases. The usefulness of supervision to the supervisee and the potential for liability may depend on the student's ability to select appropriate and representative cases for supervision review. In either case, at a public university, all clients must be considered as "real" clients, and services should be provided consistent with standards of professional practice.

Mental Health Emergencies

Whenever clients are seen for counseling, the potential for emergencies exists. Hence, all clinics need a clear, specific set of mental health emergency procedures that are articulated to all staff and students using the facility. The procedures should be in writing and reviewed with all clinic counselors as part of training practices. The greater the degree of specificity, the less confusion will result when an emergency occurs, and the greater the degree of comfort that will be felt by the inexperienced clinician when faced with an emergency situation. Emergency procedures also will facilitate transfer of the client to an appropriate facility so that harm may be averted. Liability may increase substantially without adequate emergency procedures in place. One way to reduce liability concerns is to require all counselors on staff to have participated in a mental health emergency and suicide-prevention workshop so that they can recognize and assess lethality and be prepared to manage such a situation.

Summary

Finding "real" clients for counseling students to work with is an essential part of counseling training, and at the same time fraught with problems.

Counselor education clinics that seek to provide "real-life" clients, or even clients from undergraduate classes, immediately place themselves in the dual role of being a training clinic and a community mental health agency. These two roles may, and often do, come in conflict, requiring the best thinking of counselor educators to determine how to provide the highest level and quality of training in a realistic environment that promotes education as well as the welfare of individuals. Our ethical code clearly states that the premier responsibility each of us has is to our client, and this responsibility does not change just because the setting is one that would not exist if not for its training function.

Implications

1. The Association for Counselor Education and Supervision (ACES), counselors educators, and the American Counseling Association (ACA) Ethics Committee need to begin dialogue concerning the issues discussed here relative to counselor-training clinics. How to get "real" clients for counseling practice while providing the highest quality of service with the needs of the client as the primary consideration needs to be addressed.

2. Conguence between the mission of the counselor education department (i.e., training) and the mission of the clinic (i.e., training and services) must be carefully considered as integral to the best possible service to all publics, students, as well as clients. Counselors and counselor educators will find it helpful to examine their priorities for training and services, and to compare individual perceptions of appropriate missions with the stated mission and operating policies of the on-campus clinic.

3. Sample policy and procedure statements, particularly those that have been scrutinized by legal counsel, are an increasingly relevant need. Counselor education programs wishing to establish clinics would benefit from concrete examples, as would those with existing programs that would like to improve their clinical-training laboratories.

References

Chi Sigma Iota/National Board for Certified Counselors. (1989). *Client rights and responsibilities.* Greensboro, NC: Authors.

CONCLUSION:
WHERE TO NEXT?

CHAPTER 21

CONCLUDING THOUGHTS: COUNSELING LABORATORIES IN THE FUTURE

Joseph C. Rotter

This final chapter, or afterthought, is a reflection on the need for counselor educators to continue to study carefully the feasibility of implementing standards for directors of counselor education laboratories and clinics. Members of the Association for Counselor Education and Supervision (ACES) Directors of Clinical Training and Clinics Interest Network and other invited contributors, through the "Think Tank" held during the 1992 ACES National Conference in San Antonio, Texas, contributed the chapters included in this book. Considerable study and thought went into both the "Think Tank" and the previous chapters.

These contributions to the limited literature available addressing counselor education laboratories have confirmed the need to study further this most important aspect of counselor education. Is it not interesting that this most important aspect has been left as one of the final vestiges to the standards for counselor preparation? Could it be that those who preceded us did not find the clinical training of counselors to be imperative? Were they less sophisticated than we when it comes to what constitutes good practice? I think the answer to both of these questions is no. I suspect that writing about counselor education laboratories was left unattended for the many reasons outlined in the pages that preceded this chapter. The need and desire were there, and many training laboratories were operational, but somehow counselor educators have neither discussed nor studied on-campus laboratory training until now. Furthermore, from a historical perspective, much of what is now counselor education was a backlash to existing forms of training and practice in the other mental health professions, which, as stated in chapter 1, had their own ideas regarding on-campus clinical training.

Historically, there has been resistance among counselor educators to "credentialing" for fear of boxing people out of the market (note the early relationships of counselors with psychologists and present-day encounters with marriage and family therapists). Perhaps it was this resistance that prevented counselor educators from being more prescriptive in their training models. If this were true initially, we have (although questionably) become more rigid and recognize the risks in not having standards of preparation and practice.

Another possible reason for the limited emphasis on counselor education laboratories is that, as a new profession, models of effective practice, although available, were not categorized or consistently delivered. Again, it must be emphasized that isolated examples and models of comprehensive counselor education labs have been in place for some time. However, as has been pointed out in this publication, many practices have not been shared in print. Perhaps this is a function of those who are in the trenches designing and implementing time-consuming laboratories. If one's time is spent focusing on the day-to-day mechanics of managing an effective clinic, one does not have the time to write. Some of these reasons or excuses may appear to be strawhouse notions, but collectively with other reasons could have had, and continue to have, an impact on the paucity of literature and research in this area.

CACREP Standards

Clearly the authors of the inclusive chapters of this book have concluded that the Council for Accreditation of Counseling and Related Educational Programs (CACREP) standards need to address more clinical experiences in counselor preparation. However, without a clear understanding of what constitutes an effective clinic, such standards cannot be written. This book has provided select models of delivery. It is clear that further flushing out of models is imperative. One next step for ACES and the Directors of Clinical Training and Clinics Interest Network, which is currently underway, per Myers and Smith (chapter 1), is to survey the many counselor education programs across the country to determine which programs have clinical laboratories and identify the models that they use to provide training. There may not be one right approach, or the right approach may not exist at present. Collectively reviewed and studied, perhaps examples of effective practice could be made available for replication.

On- or Off-Campus Clinics?

With all due respect to the authors who have contributed to this publication, it is possible that the conclusion that on-campus clinics are superior to off-campus settings is but a bias of those who have been actively involved in on-campus laboratories. Simply stated, the issue is not whether the clinic is on or off campus. The issue has to do with quality control. We in academia are often accused of being arrogant and out of touch with the real world. If this can be proved, then on-campus clinics might be inconsistent with real-world issues and practice. However, if the contrary is true—that "real-world practices" (i.e., off-campus training) represent a lack of concern for research and development—then counselors in training may not be exposed to advancements in the profession.

The university setting is one place in our society with a stated purpose for discourse, a search for truth, and the establishment of new knowledge and practice. This is not to say that new knowledge is not generated outside of the university, but that it is not the stated purpose of most off-campus counseling settings.

It is apparent that significant data do not exist to put this argument to rest. Perhaps this is another area of study for the ACES Network. Perhaps it is possible that an ideal might exist that combines on- and off-campus laboratories; or better yet, some form that does not yet have a prototype. One can get excited about such potential.

With current and future (as yet unknown) technology, there is no limit to how we might better educate counselors. Real-time experiences without the risks inherent in today's methods are within our reach. Distance learning and interactive computer technology are at our fingertips. Not long from now we will perhaps look back on our current practices in the most sophisticated models presented in this book as quite primitive and in fact frightening. As pointed out by several and implied by others, what we do today in the name of clinical experiences is inherent with risk. This is probably due to inconsistency in preclinic preparation, supervision, and evaluation. As trite and overused as the term *quality control* is, it is at the center of concern over these issues.

Reliance on technology to get us out of this quagmire is of course too simple. There are some intrinsic and immediate problems that need to be addressed. In fact, a case can be made for the termination of all clinical practices until a safe model is developed—all of the authors in this publication cited problems with their models. However, this approach is not practical. What we have in place is better (albeit from our professional judgment) than no supervised experience at all. If we can ensure the safety of the client at the same level of the seasoned practitioner, we must continue to expose our trainees to the "best practices." Herein lies the problem: What constitutes "best practices"? The few models presented in this book are all flawed to the extent that they rely on the competency of those in charge. Thus, the need is for standards for training those who will be in charge: the clinic directors and counselor supervisors.

Standards now exist for the training of counselor supervisors (Association for Counselor Education and Supervision, Supervision Interest Network, 1990). In reading these standards, Item 6.7 states that the supervisor "uses supervisory methods appropriate to the counselor's level of conceptual development, training and experience." This judgment by the supervisor could be the determining factor for placement in a laboratory experience.

Perhaps standards for clinical directors need to be established. However, we need to be careful not to overstandardize the profession for fear that we could thwart creativity and limit access.

The relationship between theory and practice, as well as the student's ability to integrate these two phases of counselor education, are critical to the extent to which subsequent independent learning occurs. Measures of competence or assessment of outcomes need to be considered when placing students in a clinical setting, be it on or off campus.

Another practical issue determining the use of in-house or field clinical experiences is whether the institution has a doctoral program where advanced students can assist under supervision with the supervision of entry-level students. The programs described in this publication are at doctoral-granting institutions. Master's-level-only institutions, where most counselors are trained, generally do not have the luxury of advanced students to provide supervision—another issue for the ACES Network.

Dream On

Perhaps an expanded version of the Southern Illinois University clinic, which integrates allied professional training programs to include off-campus sites, would provide opportunities for "real-world" experiences while ensuring quality control. The university would have an on-campus clinic with satellite or affiliate centers in the community. As part of their load, faculty would be assigned to either the campus or satellite center for supervision. Again, with the advancing technology, the actual physical appearance of the faculty member may not be necessary at the centers. Telenetworking of the facilities could overcome the barriers of distance and time. Who knows, maybe this model is already in place and all we need to do is find it.

Conclusion

The conclusion to all that has been addressed during the ACES think tank and in this book is that we need to do more investigation of "best practices" and disseminate effective certifiable models of clinical instruction for counselors. Once these models have been identified and studied, perhaps then a process of review and certification would be appropriate.

For those of us who have been in the profession for many years, it has become notable that we are continually growing. This study of clinical instruction is another sign of our growth. Those who have contributed to this beginning are to be commended for their dedication to the improvement of the education of counselors.

References

Association for Counselor Education and Supervision, Supervision Interest Network. (1990). Standards for counseling supervisors. *Journal of Counseling and Development, 69,* 30–32.

APPENDICES

1988 CACREP STANDARDS FOR CLINICAL TRAINING

SECTION III
CLINICAL INSTRUCTION

Clinical instruction includes laboratory experiences, practicum, and internships which are taken throughout a student's program.

A. Regular, adjunct, and affiliate program faculty who provide on-campus individual and/or group practicum and/or internship supervision:

1. hold doctoral degrees in counselor education or a closely related professional specialty or are receiving supervision from a doctoral-level person holding a degree in counselor education.
2. have relevant professional experience and have demonstrated competence in counseling and/or human development at levels appropriate for the students supervised.

B. Students serving as individual and/or group practicum and/or internship supervisors:

1. have completed at least **two** (2) practica and **one** (1) internship equivalent to those within the entry-level program.
2. are themselves supervised by program faculty.

C. On-site (e.g., off-campus) practicum and/or internship supervisors for the program:

1. have a minimum of a Master's Degree in the program emphasis area and possess appropriate certifications and/or licenses.
2. have a minimum of **two** (2) years of pertinent professional experience.

3. have been apprised of the program's expectations, requirements, and evaluation procedures for students in practica and/or internship.

D. Facilities for supervised individual and/or group prepracticum and practicum experiences are available in a coordinated counseling laboratory setting which is conducive to modeling and demonstration. It is under the direct control of the institution's academic unit in which the program is housed and includes, but is not limited to the following:

   1. individual counseling rooms, with assured privacy and sufficient space for appropriate equipment (e.g., videotape and audiotape).
   2. rooms for small group work, with assured privacy and sufficient space for appropriate equipment.
   3. portable and permanent audio- and videotape recording, and playing equipment.
   4. rooms with one-way vision glass.
   5. acoustical (i.e., sound reduction) treatment throughout.
   6. exemplary, current professional resources including career, leisure, and occupational information materials, standardized tests and interpretation aids, and microcomputer equipment.

E. Technical assistance for the use and maintenance of audio- and videotape, and microcomputer equipment is available.

F. In order to improve supervised clinical experiences for students in the program, the program faculty engages in program development outreach including, but not limited to:

   1. provision of in-service activities for counseling and human development practitioners.
   2. provision of opportunities for students in the program to assist with professional in-service education and other professional development activities.

G. The program faculty provides orientation, assistance and consultation to off-campus practicum and internship supervisors.

If accreditation is sought for an entry-level program in Community Counseling, School Counseling, or Student Affairs Practice in Higher Education with a *counseling* emphasis, the required minimum practicum is a *counseling* practicum and the required minimum internship is a *counseling* internship. The standards for *counseling* practicum and internship are presented below. If accreditation is sought for an entry-level program in Student Affairs Practice in Higher Education with a Developmental or Administrative emphasis, the required minimum practicum is a *student affairs* practicum and the required minimum internship is a *student affairs* internship, encompassing student affairs knowledge and skills and on-site supervision. The Developmental or Administrative program emphasis practicum and internship standards incorporate some modifications of the counseling practicum and internship standards presented below; see Environmental and Specialty Standards for Student Affairs Practice in Higher Education (pg. 41) for these modifications. If accreditation is sought for an entry-level program in *Mental Health Counseling*, the practicum and internship clock hours for this program emphasis incorporate some modifications of the standards presented below; see Environmental and Specialty Standards for Mental Health Counseling (pg. 37), Clinical Instruction (pg. 51) for these modifications.

H. The program requires students to complete supervised practicum(s) that total a minimum of 100 clock hours. The practicum(s) provide(s) for the development of individual and group counseling skills under supervision. The practicum(s) provide(s) an opportunity to perform, on a limited basis and under supervision, some of the activities that a regularly employed staff member in the setting would be expected to perform. A regularly employed staff member is defined as a person occupying the professional role to which the student is aspiring. The student's practicum:

1. includes a minimum of 40 hours of direct service work with clientele appropriate to the program emphasis.
2. allows the student to gain supervised experience in individual and group interactions with clientele appropriate to the program emphasis.
3. includes minimum of **one** (1) hour per week of individual supervision by a program faculty member supervisor or a student

supervisor working under the supervision of a program faculty member.

4. includes a minimum of **one and one-half** (1½) hours per week of group supervision with other students in similar practica or internships by a program faculty member supervisor or a student supervisor working under supervision by a program faculty member.

5. allows the student to become familiar with a variety of professional activities other than direct service work.

6. allows the student to obtain audio- and/or videotapes for use in supervision, of the student's interactions with clientele appropriate to the program emphasis area.

7. allows the student to gain supervised experience in the use of a variety of professional resources such as appraisal instruments, computers, print and non-print media, professional literature, and research.

8. includes formal evaluation of the student's performance during the practicum by the program faculty member supervisor.

9. is, if possible and appropriate, commensurate with state (counselor) licensure and/or certification practicum requirements applicable in the state in which the program is housed.

I. The program requires students to complete a supervised internship (or, in the case of Student Affairs Practice in Higher Education, equivalent experiences) of 600 clock hours, which is begun only after successful completion of the student's practicum (as defined in H above). The internship provides an opportunity for the student to perform all the activities that a regularly employed staff member in the setting would be expected to perform. A regularly employed staff member is defined as a person occupying the professional role to which the student is aspiring. The student's internship:

1. includes a minimum of 240 hours of direct service work with clientele appropriate to the program emphasis area.

2. includes a minimum of **one** (1) hour per week of individual supervision.

3. includes a minimum of **one and one-half** (1½) hours per week of group supervision.

4. allows the student to become familiar with a variety of professional activities other than direct service work.

5. allows the student to obtain audio- and/or videotapes, for use in supervision, of the student's interactions with clientele appropriate to the program emphasis area.
6. allows the student to gain supervised experience in the use of a variety of professional resources such as appraisal instruments, computers, print and non-print media, professional literature, and research.
7. includes formal evaluation of the student's performance during the internship by a program faculty member supervisor.
8. is, if possible and appropriate, commensurate with the state (counselor) licensure and/or certification internship requirements applicable in the state in which the program is housed.

J. The practicum and internship experiences are tutorial forms of instruction; therefore, the individual supervision of five students is considered equivalent to the teaching of **one** three-semester hour course. Such a ratio is considered maximum.

K. The within-an-academic-term student to faculty ratio for practicum or internship seminars should not be greater than 10:1 for each three-semester or equivalent quarter credit hours of faculty member load assignment.

L. Students formally evaluate their supervisors at the conclusions of their practica or internships.

M. Students are strongly encouraged to have professional liability insurance prior to participation in practicum or internship experiences.

1994 CACREP STANDARDS FOR CLINICAL TRAINING

SECTION III
CLINICAL INSTRUCTION

Clinical instruction includes supervised practica and internships completed within a student's program of study. Practicum and internship requirements are considered to be the most critical experience elements in the program.

A. Each regular, adjunct, and affiliate program faculty member who provides on-campus individual and/or group practicum and/or internship supervision has the following:

1. a doctoral degree from a program in counselor education or a closely related field or is receiving supervision from such a person;

2. relevant professional experience and demonstrated competence in counseling and/or human development at levels appropriate for the students supervised; and

3. relevant training and supervision experience.

B. Students serving as individual and/or group practicum supervisors:

1. have completed practicum and internship experiences equivalent to those within the entry-level program;

2. have completed or are receiving training in counseling supervision; and

3. are themselves supervised by program faculty with a faculty/student ratio of 1:5.

C. A site supervisor should meet the following criteria:

    1. a minimum of a master's degree in counseling or a closely related field and appropriate certifications and/or licenses;

    2. a minimum of two (2) years of pertinent professional experience; and

    3. knowledge of the program's expectations, requirements, and evaluation procedures for students.

D. A counseling laboratory that is conducive to modeling, demonstration, and training is available and used for clinical instruction. Administrative control of the laboratory facility allows adequate and appropriate access by the program. The laboratory facility includes, but is not limited to, the following:

    1. rooms for individual counseling, with assured privacy and sufficient space for appropriate equipment (e.g., videotape and audiotape);

    2. rooms for small group work, with assured privacy and sufficient space for appropriate equipment;

    3. portable and permanent audio and videotape recording and playback equipment;

    4. rooms with observational capabilities; and

    5. acoustical (i.e., sound reduction) treatment throughout.

E. Technical assistance for the use and maintenance of audio and videotape and microcomputer equipment is available.

F. The program faculty provides orientation, assistance, and consultation to supervisors.

G. In order to improve supervised clinical experiences for students in the program, the program faculty provide professional development opportunities for site supervisors (e.g., training in supervision, crisis intervention).

H. The program requires students to complete supervised practicum experiences that total a minimum of 100 clock hours. The practicum provides for the development of individual counseling and group work skills under supervision. The student's practicum includes the following:

1. a minimum of 40 hours of direct service with clients, so that experience can be gained in individual and group interactions (at least one-fourth of these hours should be in group work);
2. a minimum of one (1) hour per week of individual supervision (using audiotape, videotape, and/or direct observation) over a minimum of one academic term by a program faculty member or a supervisor working under the supervision of a program faculty member;
3. a minimum of one and one-half (1½) hours per week of group supervision with other students in similar practica over a minimum of one academic term by a program faculty member or a supervisor under the supervision of a program faculty member; and
4. evaluation of the student's performance throughout the practicum including a formal evaluation at the completion of the practicum.

I. The program requires students to complete a supervised internship of 600 clock hours that is begun after successful completion of the student's practicum (as defined in Standard III.H). Consideration should be given to selecting internship sites that offer opportunities for students to engage in both individual counseling and group work. The internship provides an opportunity for the student to perform under supervision a variety of activities that a regularly employed staff member in the setting would be expected to perform. A regularly employed staff member is defined as a person occupying the professional role to which the student is aspiring. The student's internship includes the following:

1. a minimum of 240 hours of direct service with clients appropriate to the program of study;
2. a minimum of one (1) hour per week of individual supervision, throughout the internship, usually performed by the on-site supervisor;
3. a minimum of one and one-half (1½) hours per week of group supervision, throughout the internship, usually performed by a program faculty member supervisor;
4. the opportunity for the student to become familiar with a variety of professional activities other than direct service;

5. the opportunity for the student to develop audio and/or video-tapes of the student's interactions with clients appropriate to the specialization for use in supervision;

6. the opportunity for the student to gain supervised experience in the use of a variety of professional resources such as assessment instruments, computers, print and nonprint media, professional literature, research, and information and referral to appropriate providers; and

7. a formal evaluation of the student's performance during the internship by a program faculty supervisor in consultation with the site supervisor.

J. The practicum and internship experiences are tutorial forms of instruction; therefore, when the individual supervision is provided by program faculty, the ratio of 5 students to 1 faculty member is considered equivalent to the teaching of one (1) three-semester hour course. Such a ratio is considered maximum.

K. Group supervision seminars for practicum and internship should not exceed 10 students.

L. Clinical experiences (practicum and internship) provide opportunities for students to counsel clients representative of the ethnic, lifestyle, and demographic diversity of their community.

M. Students formally evaluate their supervisors at the conclusion of their practicum and internship experiences.

N. Students are strongly encouraged to have professional liability insurance prior to participation in practicum or internship experiences.

GLOSSARY OF TERMS RELEVANT TO CLINICAL TRAINING, 1988 STANDARDS

Internship—a distinctly defined, post-practicum, supervised curricular experience intended to enable the student to refine and enhance basic counseling (or student affairs) skills, develop more advanced counseling (or student affairs) skills, and integrate professional knowledge and skills appropriate to the student's initial postgraduation professional placement.

Laboratory—a curricular experience which provides both observation and participation in specific activities. Laboratory experiences may be offered throughout the preparatory program (e.g., through role-playing, listening to tapes, viewing videotape playbacks, testing, organizing and using personnel records, interviewing field practitioners, preparing and examining case studies, and/or using career information materials).

Practicum—a distinctly defined, pre-internship, supervised curricular experience intended to enable the student to develop basic counseling (or student affairs) skills and integrate professional knowledge and skills appropriate to the student's program emphasis.

Supervision—a tutorial form of instruction wherein a supervisor assigned to the student's program emphasis monitors the student's activities in practicum or internship and facilitates the student's practicum or internship and facilitates the student's practicum or internship learning and skill development experiences.

GLOSSARY OF TERMS RELEVANT TO CLINICAL TRAINING, 1994 STANDARDS

Clinical Instruction—all supervised coursework within which the student has the opportunity to engage in a broad range of clinical activities similar to those performed by a professional counselor. This includes all practica and internships completed within a student's program.

Internship—a distinctly defined, post-practicum, supervised clinical experience intended to enable the student to refine and enhance basic counseling or student development skills, and integrate professional knowledge and skills appropriate to the student's specialization and initial postgraduation professional placement.

Practicum—a distinctly defined, supervised clinical experience intended to enable the student to develop basic counseling skills and integrate professional knowledge. Practicum is offered prior to the internship.

Supervision—a tutorial form of instruction wherein a supervisor assigned to the student's program monitors the student's activities in practicum or internship and facilitates the student's practicum or internship learning and skill development experiences.

Note. The term "counseling laboratory" is not defined in the glossary to the 1994 standards.

SAMPLE CLIENT RECRUITMENT LETTER AND FLYER, WRIGHT STATE UNIVERSITY

Institution's Letterhead

Current Date

Samaritan Health Center
232 Mental Health Drive
Dayton, Ohio 45406-1891

Dear Clinical Director:

RE: WSU Office for Counseling and Life Planning Services (OCLPS)

Wright State University's Office for Counseling and Life Planning Services provides services for persons needing career and/or personal/social counseling. Assistance with relationship, adjustment and behavioral problems, outplacement, career counseling, resume creation, and job interview skills are just some of the services provided by the OCLPS.

In addition, evaluations—used for a variety of purposes—are also available. These assessments can reveal occupational interests, job suitability, personality strengths, values, "windows of opportunity," and areas needing improvement within individuals.

At the OCLPS, we're dedicated to helping individuals and groups clarify their goals and expand their options. Our comprehensive services are based on a sliding-fee scale. Licensed Professional Counselor (LPC) and Licensed Professional Clinical Counselor (LPCC) trainees (graduate students from the Department of Human Services) work under the auspices of licensed mental health providers.

Please inform your personnel of our services. You are encouraged to reproduce and distribute the enclosed flyer. Additional copies are available upon request. In addition, our staff is available for presentations.

Feel free to telephone us at (513) 873-2299 if we can be of assistance to you and your organization.

Best regards,

Richard A. Wantz, EdD, NCC
Associate Professor
Director and Psychologist
OCLPS

Susan K. Spille
Graduate Clinic Coordinator—
 OCLPS LPC Trainee

Attachment

Office for Counseling and Life Planning Services
M091, Music Wing, Lower Level, Creative Arts Building
Department of Human Services
College of Education and Human Services
Wright State University

The Office for Counseling and Life Planning Services (OCLPS) offers personal, social, and career counseling to individuals and families. Referrals are accepted from schools, corporations, government and military installations, businesses, churches, and organizations. Clients are assessed a fee on a sliding-scale basis.

The OCLPS is a teaching facility for the counselor education program. The clinic enables graduate students to integrate and apply theory with practice. A secondary purpose includes providing assistance to individuals from the metropolitan community. *Our current waiting list is not long, and referrals are welcome.*

The OCLPS offers the following services:

Counseling—assistance for individuals and families experiencing personal, relationship, marital, adjustment, or parenting problems; stress; low self-esteem; depression; or grief. A personal growth group is offered for healthy individuals seeking self-actualization.

Career Counseling—individual and group services focusing on career decision making and outplacement, occupational information, and lifestyle assistance. Support groups for unemployed individuals and displaced homemakers are offered.

Assessment—evaluation of interests, values, preferences, needs, skills, abilities, aptitudes, and personality dimensions through a complete range of surveys and inventories. In addition, clients receive detailed information regarding how these attributes relate to occupational success and personal growth. Our document scanner and computer enables quick, thorough, and accurate scoring and interpretation of appraisal instruments.

Self-Marketing Strategies for Clients with Career Concerns—creating opportunities, networking, telephone skills, interviewing strategies, effective resume creation, written communications, follow-up, asking for referrals, salary negotiation, and selecting and accepting the best offer.

Empowerment—creating a winning mental set; building skill and confidence; capitalizing on strengths and compensating for weaknesses; setting goals and establishing priorities; organizing, planning, and preparing for success; managing stress, tasks, people, and time; handling rejection; overcoming procrastination; and developing positive thinking skills.

For additional information, or to schedule an appointment, call (513) 873-2299.

A MODEL OF CASE CONCEPTUALIZATION

A MODEL FOR CASE CONCEPTUALIZATION

by Susan A. Neufeldt

I. Sources of information
   A. Clinical interview
   B. Formal assessments
   C. Impressions/reports of others
   D. Personal reaction of the therapist

II. The nature of the problem
   A. Present concern
      1. Client's description of problem
      2. What has precipitated the client's coming in now?
   B. What historical factors in this person's life have contributed to the problem?
   C. What cultural and social factors contribute to the problem?
      1. Cultural background
      2. History of social oppression
   D. What personal characteristics and behaviors produce the problem in life for the client?
   E. What personal resources does the client bring to bear on the problem?
      1. Usual coping strategies
      2. Personal strengths
      3. Personal deficits
   F. Counselor's hypothesis about the nature of the problem(s) the client faces

III. Nature of initial contract
   A. Specified focus, if there is one
   B. Time constraints based on imminence of issue, perons' availability, counselor's availability, setting constraints, and financial resources

IV. Goals for treatment
   A. Depth of focus agreed on by client and therapist
      1. First-order focus—relatively minor change to parts of a system (tend to be goal oriented and instrumental in emphasis)
      2. Second-order focus—involves a transformation of the entire system, structurally and functionally, more ambiguity and risk (process level)
   B. Statement of goals

V. Change strategy
   A. Theory of human change
   B. Match between person and change strategy
      1. Personality and cultural background of client
      2. Appropriateness of strategy for agreed goals
      3. Time/resource constraints
   C. Arenas of change
      1. In sessions
      2. Outside of sessions
   D. Therapist's responsibilities, delineated by therapist
   E. Client's responsibilities, agreed to by client
   F. Predicted obstacles and tests of the therapist

VI. Desired outcomes
   A. Insights and understanding
   B. Behaviors

SAMPLE CLIENT RECRUITMENT FLYER, UNIVERSITY OF NORTH CAROLINA AT GREENSBORO

Services Provided

Individual Counseling, Group Counseling and Support

For persons experiencing a range of life concerns, such as relationship concerns, family issues, self-esteem and self-efficacy, work, leisure and retirement concerns, weight-loss problems, fears and phobias, or other issues, CCS offers services from a perspective of respect and care for the individual. Group counseling and support are used when concerns are best addressed through interaction with peers.

Marriage and Family Counseling

CCS addresses issues facing couples and families, from relationship enrichment concerns to short-term solution-oriented therapy. Examples include acting-out youth, communication difficulties, substance abuse recovery issues (postdetox only), parent–child difficulties, and troubled marriages.

Older Adults Counseling

Older adults face issues unique to them, such as changing family and friendship relations, changes in body functioning, time use after retirement, relating to a spouse, and changes in financial status. CCS staff trained specifically in older adult concerns provide quality services.

Career Counseling and Life-Career Development

Many persons wish to establish a new and satisfying career, to make an effective career transition, or to get more satisfaction from balancing life-career roles. CCS provides comprehensive career counseling and consulting.

Grief and Loss Counseling

Transitions of life such as death, divorce, retirement, moving, children leaving home, pet loss, and others may produce a need to grieve and cope with the loss. CCS provides caring, understanding, and awareness of the adjustments needed in difficult transitions.

Stress Management

Life's difficulties may frequently induce stress reactions. CCS provides stress-reduction counseling as well as stress-prevention counseling.

Educational Counseling

For adolescents, college students, and adults who face difficulty in motivation, test anxiety, classroom anxiety, or academic performance.

Counseling and Consulting Services offers services on a sliding-fee scale. For more information, or to make a referral, contact:

Gerald Hutchinson, Jr., MEd, NCC
Intake Counselor and Assistant
 Clinic Coordinator
(919) 334-5112

Jane E. Myers, PhD, NCC
Clinic Coordinator and
 Professor
(919) 334-5100

Counseling and Consulting Services
The University of North Carolina at Greensboro 1000 Spring Garden St. Greensboro, NC 27412